Table of Contents

Introduction

Regardless of the type of work you do, whether you are an accountant or an actor, a zookeeper or a Zen instructor, you can improve your job performance by understanding the different types of intelligence and then striving to increase your core intelligence in those areas which are essential to your specific type of job.

While increasing your intelligence level does not happen overnight, this book will give you helpful information on heightening creativity, improving concentration, boosting productivity and expanding your abilities in many other areas of thinking. You will learn to identify your individual strengths and weaknesses, and find new ways to build upon the positives, while minimizing the negatives. Additionally, we will look at some of the factors that interfere with the ability to effectively perform a variety of tasks, and ways to eliminate those factors, so that you can reach your full potential on the job.

Before beginning to increase intelligence, however, it is important to have a firm grasp of the brain functions and cognitive skills involved in the application of what is commonly referred to as intelligence. A strong understanding of the different types of intelligence, and how each one can be used in every day work and life settings, is also essential for a successful and productive experience.

What is Intelligence?

Many different authors have attempted to define the meaning of the word intelligence. In the most general sense, intelligence can be summed up as a level of mental aptitude or acuteness. When we use our intelligence, we draw on the ability to reason, to solve problems and to apply acquired knowledge logically, in a way that is appropriate to whatever situation we are in at the time.

Modern scientists attempt to measure intelligence by using a variety of different testing methods. The most widely recognized test of intelligence is the "IQ test", or "Intelligence Quotient Test". This test contains several different parts, each designed to measure a certain aspect of brain function. The test most commonly uses two separate scales ("Wechsler Adult Intelligence Scale"), to gather information about the test subject's ability to process, organize, understand and apply information. The scales measure the subject's ability to process information on a "verbal scale" as well as a "performance scale". The verbal scale test consists mainly of oral questions, while the performance scale test is geared toward visual and kinetic processes.

Looking at the "Wechsler Adult Intelligence Scale" we can begin to get some insight into the mental processes which are evaluated by the "IQ test", to determine an individual's overall intelligence level. These mental processes include:

Verbal Scale Measures:

1. Memory

2. Knowledge

3. Calculating ability

4. Problem-solving ability

5. Abstract thinking ability

6. Speed of mental processing

7. Planning skills

8. Spatial Orientation

Performance Scale measures include: the ability to think logically, follow patterns, complete sequences, assess similarities and differences, interpret symbols and make inferences regarding spatial recognition.

Most standard IQ tests will also attempt to measure the subject's level of distraction, which in turn means that the ability to focus and concentrate on a given task is also an essential part of the intelligence measure.

While many scientists question the IQ test's ability to accurately measure intelligence, by looking closely at the scales used in the testing process, we can begin to get some idea of what is actually meant by the term "intelligence."

Rather than thinking of intelligence as a single subject, the most helpful information can be obtained by viewing it as multiple subjects. Consider the appearance of a finished jigsaw puzzle. When you stand back and look at it, it seems to be a whole - yet that whole was created from many different, complex parts. Each part plays an important role in the finished picture. Without examining each part during the building process, it would also have been impossible to have a clear understanding of the finished project. In order to understand intelligence, we need to examine the many brain functions and processes that are used to define it, as well as the ones that we most need to increase to improve it.

Right and Left Brain

The human brain is divided into two hemispheres. Unlike your two eyes, ears, hands and feet, however, the two hemispheres of the brain perform very different functions.

The left brain is highly logical, handling tasks such as organizing, planning, sequencing, and calculating. It also stores data and factual information. This is known as your "thinking brain" or your "logical brain".

The right side of the brain is considered to be the "creative brain". It handles art, music, poetry and drama. This side of the brain also handles our emotions, and can give us insight, intuition and imagination. When we are spiritually active, as when we are deep in prayer or meditation, the right side of our brain is also at work.

A standard "IQ test" is geared toward measuring left brain function, yet when we consider that there are many important processes handled by the right brain, including our ability to think creatively and to solve problems intuitively, we cannot simply discount the importance of right brain function. What's more, the right brain allows us to imagine, to invent, to conceive new ideas and to be innovative in our approach to work and life. Finally, because the right brain is the emotional center of our bodies, both our motivation and our emotional connectedness to whatever we are doing is maintained in this area of the brain. When we consider intelligence then, it is important to look at both right and left brain functions, to get a well-rounded view of what constitutes intelligence.

Types of Intelligence

One of the most important and frequently quoted works on intelligence *"Frames of Mind"* was published by Psychologist Howard Gardner, in 1983. In his book, Gardner categorizes areas of intelligence into seven main types. His work includes both right and left brain processes, and describes how each type of intelligence is important in both professional and everyday life.

Verbal Intelligence: the ability to use language to speak and write clearly, to comprehend words and their meanings, whether spoken or written; the ability to store and appropriately use vocabulary. *If you have never taken a verbal intelligence assessment test, you might want to try the free assessment tool from Queendom.com.

Visual Intelligence: The brain's ability to construct and replicate visual images, recognize and identify images, process and organize visual elements and connect visual elements to other areas of the brain i.e. language, sensory knowledge, emotional response etc...*If you would like to assess your visual intelligence level visit similarminds.com to take a free visual/spatial intelligence test.

Physical Intelligence (or kinesthetic intelligence): Includes balance, body coordination, ease and speed of movement, dexterity, eye-hand coordination, as well as the ability to carry out intricate tasks. Can also include sensory reactions to touch and feel, as well as intuitive type bodily reactions to emotions, events, or both real and perceived dangers or threats.

Musical and Rhythmic Intelligence: Musical ability, or the ability to enjoy or appreciate music and/or various rhythms.*A unique online test from Jakemandell.com offers insight into assessing your visual/musical intelligence.

Mathematical Intelligence: Mathematical and Scientific reasoning abilities, the ability to think logically, to understand, analyze and process numbers, data and statistical information, to solve problems, identify patterns and comprehend abstract analysis and functions. *To assess your mathematical intelligence visit alliqtests.com.

Introspective Intelligence: Self reflection and self-awareness, the quest for deeper meaning, analyzing spiritual and philosophical ideas, understanding and acknowledgment of the inner self.

Interpersonal Intelligence: The ability to connect with others, experience empathy, to understand other viewpoints, communicate effectively and listen attentively.

Gardner later added an eighth form of intelligence to his initial list, that of natural intelligence. This intelligence can be found in the ability to understand and connect with nature and your natural surroundings.

The most successful individual's are able to draw on multiple types of intelligence, rather than focus entirely on one or two types. While you may be a mathematical genius, if you have little or no interpersonal intelligence, you will no doubt still have trouble finding success in your chosen field. Literacyworks.org provides a simple test for helping you determine your top three intelligences, as well as to identify areas where you may need to make some improvement.

Contrary to popular belief, it is possible to increase your intelligence level by focusing on one or more of the areas mentioned above.

Crystallized and Fluid Intelligence

The "Cattel-Horn theory of intelligence" approaches the subject from a different, but relevant, point of view. This theory further divides intelligence into the two categories mentioned above, crystallized and fluid.

Fluid intelligence exists independently of previous knowledge or education. When using fluid intelligence a person is able to approach a problem with no preexisting concepts or ideas regarding the outcome. Fluid intelligence, then, is the ability to formulate an approach to the unknown.

Crystallized intelligence, on the other hand, addresses the ability to apply previously acquired knowledge and insight to a problem, using that existing information to formulate a solution to either a new or previously encountered problem.

Intelligence Versus Knowledge

Acquiring new knowledge is fundamental to building some types of intelligence, but not every type of intelligence can be strengthened by gathering new knowledge.

Knowledge can be viewed as the ideas and facts we have gathered from school, work, training, family and life experiences. Intelligence, however, deals with the ways that we learn to use that knowledge, or even to discard it, as we approach a variety of tasks, from decision making and problem solving to designing, planning, creating or performing some other work-related function.

Foreword

Now that we have gained a better understanding of the many different types of intelligence, we can begin to look at ways for increasing intelligence in these, and other areas of thinking.

Whether you are looking to boost creativity, think with greater clarity, improve memory function or strengthen interpersonal skills, this book will introduce you to the most effective methods of increasing intelligence in these and many other areas.

While each chapter seeks to address ways to improve intelligence and ability in those areas commonly needed for success in a business environment, the information can be applied to other areas of life as well. Students, volunteers, jobseekers as well as those who are otherwise interested in bettering themselves by increasing their intelligence will find this book helpful in their quest for self-improvement.

Chapter One

The Sternberg Theory of Intelligence: Implications for Adult Learning, Increased Success and Improved Work Performance

Since the 1920s several different theories on intelligence have been proposed, some widely accepted, others widely defamed. While the majority of intellectuals still prefer the "g" theory, the Sternberg Theory addresses many important issues and explains previously unexplained exceptions that the "g" theory has been unable to accurately explain.

What is the "g" theory of Intelligence?

First proposed in 1927, Charles Spearman's theory of "g" has been the basis for both standardized assessment and intelligence assessment tests, for the past several decades. In Spearman's theory, "g" represents "general knowledge", or general "IQ". It is thought to be static, and therefore it is said that a test subject's "g" factor, or basic "IQ" score will remain the same throughout his or her lifetime.

But can a subject's "IQ" score really be considered a definite indicator of success?

Sternberg Questions the Theory of "g"

In 1973 Robert Sternberg proposed a new theory of intelligence, while calling into question the many flaws associated with both the "g" model and standardized intelligence testing, in general.

In fact, it was long before 1973 that Sternberg first began to question the accuracy of the "IQ" test model. As a grade school student, Sternberg was affected by test anxiety, a condition which we now know affects a wide range of students, from elementary to college age. When Sternberg was forced to retake a standardized test with students a grade below his own level, he made up his mind to "tackle the test", only not in the way one might think.

Rather than allowing the test to assess him, Sternberg set his mind to assessing the test, and early on began to find flaws which he demonstrated by designing tests of his own. The first thing he wanted to know was how "IQ" test results were influenced by the individual test taker's level of distraction. Not surprisingly, he found that his own test scores were radically altered simply by taking the test at home, rather than in an institutional setting.

Sternberg attended both Yale and Stanford Universities, earning a PhD in Psychology. Later, after becoming an esteemed faculty member of Yale University, Sternberg published his own work on intelligence theory.

Sternberg's Theory Explained

Sternberg proposed that there are three separate and distinct levels of intelligence.

These are:

Analytical

Practical

Creative

Analytical intelligence is closest to that type of intelligence which is assessed by standardized tests as well as Intelligence Quotient tests. It consists of the ability to approach academic problems, formulate methods of solving them and apply various mental processes in order to determine a correct or logical answer. Analytical intelligence hails from that part of the brain that is able to rationalize, reason, logically process and order information.

Practical Intelligence is acquired through experience. It consists of a person's ability to adapt to a specific environment, to gain skills and improve in those skills with increasing levels of exposure. Practical intelligence is flexible, and is illustrated by the fact that the more you practice at something, the better you become at that activity. Sternberg theorized that practical intelligence cannot be taught by standardized means of education. It is an intelligence that comes from experimentation, trial and error and repeated exposure.

Creative Intelligence can be described as the ability to visualize, hypothesize, imagine, or invent new ideas or new ways to approach both known and unknown problems and tasks.

The Three Intelligences and Success

Sternberg's theory of intelligence may provide us with a better means of predicting success. His research demonstrates that the most successful individuals are not always those with the highest "g" factor. This definition explains why people with lower "IQ" scores are often highly successful in their chosen field. These individuals may have less "analytical intelligence", yet they often demonstrate a great deal of practical knowledge or creative ability.

Consider the case of a nameless young man that I once knew. He was determined by his teachers to be a "genius", after demonstrating exceptional "book smarts" and scoring very high on a standard "IQ" test. He was placed in the accelerated learning program, and was even enrolled in college courses before ever entering high school.

One day, as I was entering the library, I observed this same young man walk face first into a glass door. He was not reading, nor engaged in any other activity which would have explained his inability to logically predict that there was a door in front of him, yet he walked into it, just the same. This observation seems to demonstrate that, while a person may have a great deal of analytical intelligence, that same individual may also lack the common sense, or "practical knowledge" necessary to succeed in life.

Considering this same young man, for a moment, there are other observations to be made. While he was highly intelligent in some aspects of life, by the time he reached high school age he was considered a "social outcast" by most of his peers. Not only did he dress in inappropriately mismatched clothes, rarely comb his hair or otherwise care for his appearance, he seemed to go out of his way to offend his classmates. It seemed that almost every time someone would attempt to befriend him, he would unintentionally belittle them, or simply give off such an air of condescension that they would not approach him again. He was entirely alienated from other students, before his early graduation. Yet, even though he was shunned by the majority of his peers, in talking with him one got the sense that he saw himself as being a leader and as someone that his classmates highly esteemed.

When considering non-analytical areas of intelligence such as interpersonal and introspective, this apparent "genius" seemed lacking in both. Besides having difficulty with common everyday tasks, he had little to no social skills. He appeared to have a very skewed self-image, as well.

As a final note, this student also lacked physical strength and was not only quite uncoordinated, but appeared to be rather out of touch with his physical environment, an indicator that he may also have lacked the kind of "kinetic" intelligence that was described in the previous chapter.

Balance Equates Success

According to Sternberg's theory, the best indicator of success is balance. Individuals who demonstrate average levels of analytical, practical and creative intelligence are more likely to be successful in life than those with a disproportionate amount of any one type of intelligence.

Developing a Well Rounded Approach

You are reading this book because you want to become more intelligent. Most likely, you are also looking for ways to better your on the job performance, or even to improve your employment skills, in hopes of landing a better job in the future.

As we have seen, however, improving intelligence may not be a matter of simply increasing knowledge to get smarter. A well-rounded approach to personal growth and self-improvement is necessary, to achieve the loftier goal of increasing overall intelligence.

Assessing Your Intelligence

As a first step on your quest to becoming more intelligent, it may be best to begin with a simple, yet highly applicable use of your introspective intelligence skills. Keep in mind that there are no right or wrong answers, and that the main purpose of this activity is to gain an honest and accurate picture of those areas where you currently apply your intelligence skills, as well as those areas that you most need to focus on, to improve.

Intelligence Self-Assessment

Take a few minutes to write down the answers to the following questions:

1. What are some of the areas where you best demonstrate practical intelligence? (Describe situations that you are familiar with, comfortable in and that you feel you have a good "sense" for dealing with.)

2. What are some of the areas where you need to acquire more practical intelligence? (Situations that make you make feel uncomfortable or out of your element.)

3. Identify your best analytical abilities. (Your ability to solve problems, think logically, memorize data and facts, order, sequence, identify patterns

etc...Are you good at Math and Science?)

4. In what areas of your life are you the most creative? (Do you write, draw, paint, invent, think up new ideas etc...?)

5. In what areas of your life do you need to be more creative?

6. What interpersonal skills do you currently possess that help you succeed, both on the job and at home? (Do you have good conversational skills? Are you a good listener? Do you have strong empathy for others? Do you have a good sense of social etiquette? How well do you handle conflict etc...?)

7. Describe how your introspective intelligence skills help or hinder you in life. (Do you journal or spend time reflecting on yourself and your life? Do you have a good sense of who you are and where you want to go in the future? Do you have an appropriate level of self-confidence and self-esteem? What kind of relationship do you have with yourself? How do these things affect you in everyday life?)

8. Looking over your answers, decide which areas of intelligence you most need to focus on, to improve your life.

As you move into the next chapter of this book, keep in mind what you learned about yourself and how you apply the intelligence that you currently have to every day work situations.

Chapter Two
Increased Intelligence Realistic Approaches for Improving Analytical and Practical Intelligence

In this chapter we will look at ways to increase the three types of intelligence which Sternberg identified in his work. We will also relate some of Sternberg's ideas on intelligence to those found in the introduction of this book. To give the most accurate picture of human intelligence and how it can be improved, the concept of kinetic, introspective and interpersonal intelligences have not been entirely left out of the discussion.

While no one theory on intelligence seems to be completely accurate, a combination of viewpoints can provide a more realistic viewpoint. The chapter is divided into sections, as suggested by Sternberg, with additional information regarding other theories incorporated into the text.

This chapter also provides resources and suggested hands-on activities to help increase intelligence in one or a combination of specific areas.

How to Improve Analytical Intelligence

Analytical intelligence can be improved in a number of ways. While many people believe that they will become smarter simply by memorizing more facts and filling their minds with more trivial knowledge, this is not often true. Having a great deal of random knowledge, which has little or no real world application, does not make you intelligent. In fact, some studies suggest that memorizing facts and details in this manner can inhibit intelligent growth in many other areas. Summing it up then, unless you have a photographic memory (in which case you would probably not feel the need to read this book) approaching learning in this way can make you less intelligent, in the long run.

Our brains retain every bit of information we are exposed to, but the information is not always readily available to our conscious minds. Our ability to recall the information that we need, both quickly and effectively, largely depends on how often we use that information. Everything that we see, hear, smell, taste, read or are otherwise exposed to in our lifetime, is absorbed by the brain. As far as anyone knows none of the information ever leaves, since your mind has no eraser with which to wipe out the things you don't want or need to remember.

The brain's ability to sort and store information is potentially infinite. Yet, not all of that information is necessary in life. This is why the brain organizes and categorizes everything which it is exposed to, in the order that it subconsciously deems as most appropriate. In other words, your mind instinctively processes all the information that it takes in, prioritizing it by placing the most necessary information closest to the surface, while filtering what it considers to be the most irrelevant details downward, storing those details furthest from memory. The more often that you need to access certain details, the closer to conscious memory those details will be stored.

Knowing this, it stands to reason that the more you use your analytical intelligence, the easier it will be for you to access the areas of reasoning and higher thought needed to effectively approach analytical problems.

Things to do:

1. Solve logic problems

Regularly working through complex problems helps to train your brain to more readily perform these tasks. Visit logicproblems.org to access thousands of complex logic problems. The site provides you with a percentage for problems solved correctly, as well as a timer so that you can check your speed, as well as ability. Work to improve your overall score and to lessen the amount of time it takes for you to solve these types of problems. Once you have increased your skills, you may want to try to solve the complex logic puzzle, created by Albert Einstein, often known simply as the "goldfish test". While only an estimated 2% of the adult population has been able to solve this problem, working with it can help you increase your analytical thinking skills tremendously.

2. Work through puzzles and "brainteasers"

Look for difficult puzzles that make you think differently or look at objects in new ways. Spend some of your free time trying to solve a Rubik's Cube or using other logic manipulatives, which can help you learn analytical skills in a practical way.

3. Approach the same problem in different ways

One of the best ways to teach your brain to think more analytically is to brainstorm new and different ways of approaching the same problems or tasks. Once you have solved a difficult puzzle or complex logic problem, try to find another way to reach the same conclusion. Some experts even recommend recording yourself while solving a problem. Play back the recording and note how you approach the tasks associated with problem solving. Try to replace each initial approach with a new and different one.

4. Play sequence and memorization games

Games like "Simon", which involve remembering patterns and sequences in ever increasing order, as well as games which require visual, auditory and mental memorization, can help you increase abilities in these and other areas of analytical thinking.

5. Improve your Observation Skills

Visit spotthedifference.com. Also try the "5 differences" puzzle, available at intergames.nl.These types of games can help you gain better observational skills and learn to look more closely at the problems and situations you are faced with on the job.

6. Brainmextrix.com

This site offers a wide range of free online activities for improving analytical thinking. The site provides excellent resources for mental exercise, with each activity designed to help you increase your logic and reasoning abilities, improve the speed and accuracy of immediate recall and memory skills, heighten your ability to focus and concentrate, hone visual and observational skills, and more.

How to Improve Practical Intelligence

Practical intelligence involves learning by doing. The theory of practical intelligence suggests that to gain a good sense of how to "practically" apply a new skill to every day work or life, we must use that skill often. The more we use that skill, the better we become at using it, because the human brain learns from each exposure, and adapts to what it learns from such "trial and error" processes.

This explains why we don't always learn best by reading about, or listening to others tell us about, how to do something. If you are a hands-on type learner, one who is compelled to test things, experiment with them, or otherwise try to "see for yourself" how things work, you probably already have a good idea of how practical intelligence benefits you in everyday life.

If, on the other hand, you are used to learning by listening, reading about or otherwise being taught things by teachers, parents and other types of instructors, you may need to learn how to better use your own practical intelligence. Do you:

Fully grasp concepts when they are explained to you by others?

Have trouble applying concepts learned in school (or elsewhere) to the real world around you?

Learn best by reading, studying or memorization?

Feel intimidated by hands-on type learning experiences?

Have difficulty seeing mistakes as possible learning experiences?

Have trouble performing well in sports or other physical activities?

Give up on applying new skills if you don't master them right away?

Practical intelligence is flexible, and depends on repeated exposure to a task, situation or activity, to improve.

Things to Do

1. Take up a new hobby.

Whether it is participating in some type of sport, learning how to knit, how to draw, paint, or sculpt, just ensure that the activity is not one that you have any previous knowledge or experience in. The only other rule is that it must involve a physical activity of some type. Accept that you will not excel at this activity right away. Make up your mind to learn through trial and error. Your practical knowledge will increase as you stick with the activity. Determine for yourself that you will not quit until you have mastered the selected activity, regardless of how long it takes.

2. Set aside the instruction books and manuals

Make an effort to figure things out without the aid of guides, manuals, diagrams and other tools. Instead of reading about how to do something, examine the parts, explore the way things fit together, do it wrong, then take it apart and try again, until you finally get it right.

Other ways to improve:

a. Try to cook without recipes in front of you.

b. Assemble a jigsaw puzzle without looking at the pictures.

c. Play a game without reading the rule book first.

d. Take apart an old appliance then try to figure out how it goes back together.

e. Try orienteering, which is a lesser known sport that involves trying to find your way from one point to another, using only a compass (no maps or guidebooks allowed).

f. Go on a "survival" trip. This type of adventure requires you to learn new skills in a wilderness environment. Such an experience, while temporarily uncomfortable, can be the ultimate tool for developing practical skills in a short period of time. Most trips last from a few days up to a few weeks. The skills you develop from such an experience, however, can go a long way in helping you succeed in other areas of life.

g. Come up with our own plan. If you are used to relying on "crutches", references, resources, detailed instructions etc..., be willing to set them aside. Make it a point to increase the number of things you are able to "learn by doing."

Chapter Three
How to Improve Creative Intelligence

In the book "Creative Intelligence, Discovering the Innovative Potential in Ourselves and Others" by Alan Rowe (2002), the author proposes that there are four separate, but unique areas of creativity: intuition, inspiration (or inspirational leadership), imagination and innovation.

Understanding the Four Aspects of Creative Intelligence

Intuition can be described as an internal feeling or sense about something, which may or may not be supported by information. To get a better understanding of how intuition works to our benefit, consider the following hypothetical situation:

Example: Imagine that you work in a wholesale supply industry. One day you get a call from a previously unknown customer. He tells you that he wants to order a very large quantity of materials and that he would like you to extend him a line of credit. At first this seems like a good idea, but the more you talk with the man, the more you begin to feel that something is not right. You may not be able to say exactly why you feel that way, but you sense something suspicious or "just have a bad feeling". You turn down the order. A few days later you find out that another business down the street from yours got taken for a ride by the same man. Your intuition gave you clues about the unknown customer, while the other business owner's lack of intuition was probably what caused him to be taken advantage of.

Inspiration can be viewed as a sudden thought or internal awareness, which is often directly linked to an outside source. Inspiration happens when our mind is able to put things together in a new way. It can also occur when the brain inexplicably connects something that we are exposed to in the natural world, to something relevant to our lives.

Example: You see a stack of wood in the corner and are suddenly inspired to design a new type of shelving system. Your mind linked what it observed in the natural world to something new and unique.

Imagination might best be explained as the mind's ability to picture things which are not real, as if they were. Writers, artists, inventors etc...are able to use the powers of imagination to envision new ideas, concepts or situations in great detail.

Example: When we read a good book our minds are generally able to "envision" every aspect of the story. We say that we can "picture" everything, the appearance of the characters, the scenery, buildings, furnishings and other details of the story seem to come to life in our minds. Imagination can also help us envision characters, products, works-of-art and more, which are entirely independent of outside stimuli.

Innovation is often seen as the process of transforming abstract ideas, generated either by inspiration or imagination, into something concrete, with a real world application.

Example: You have an idea for a new board game. The process of creating that board game, writing the rules, working out the problems, designing the board, pieces and other necessary parts are all a part of the innovative process.

Ways to Improve Intuitive Intelligence

Are you familiar with your own sense of intuition? Do you trust your own judgment, and choose to "go with your gut instincts"? For many people improving their intuitive intelligence begins with learning to recognize it, then learning how to trust it.

Intuition works differently for different people. Some people describe it as either a "bad feeling" or a "good feeling". Others describe it as a "gut" feeling, one which occurs in the chest and stomach areas of the physical body. Still others say that it is like a "small voice" that spoke to them, telling them what to do or what not to do.

Developing intuition can be an introspective process. Since it is an experience that is entirely unique to each person, your best efforts to improve in this area should involve:

Things to Do

1. Getting in touch with your emotions and seeking to understand them.

2. Getting and staying in touch with your physical body. Learning to identify physical signs of intuition such as tenseness, discomfort or "gut" instincts begins with knowing how your body responds to negative and positive situations.

3. Learning to pay attention to intuitive instincts means being willing to take inventory of both body and mind, when faced with difficult decisions.

4. Think about intuitive experiences you have had in your life. Try to recall them in as much detail as possible. See if you can identify how the situations affected you physically, emotionally or otherwise. Reflecting on these experiences can help you become more in-tune to your own intuitive "voice".

5. Many people experience intuitive dreams. Before making a difficult decision, if you are not sure which way to go, give yourself time "to sleep on it." Any dreams that you have regarding the situation may be meant to give you insight regarding which direction you should take.

6. Experts on intuitive intelligence suggest that we are always using it, even though we are not always aware of it. One way that you can test this is to try to follow your vision. For example, if you are presented with two objects and are asked to pick one, the one you should choose is the one your eyes naturally look to first.

7. One of the biggest obstacles to intuitive thinking is a lack of self-confidence. People with high amounts of intuition generally exhibit a great deal of self-esteem. These people have learned how to trust their inner guidance system to help them make difficult decisions or deal with complex situations.

Ways to Improve Inspirational Intelligence

Like other forms of creative intelligence, inspiration is spontaneous, unpredictable and impossible to force. Unlike analytical concepts, or practical knowledge, inspiration is not learned by practice or increased by study and rehearsal.

Since inspiration involves our brain's ability to make connections between external and internal ideas, exposure to a wide variety of experiences and situations can serve to help develop this type of intelligence. Breaking patterns, deviating from normal routines and seeking out situations which are unfamiliar are also good ways to increase inspirational intelligence.

Things to Do

1. Visit museums and traveling art exhibits. Reflect on the ideas of the artist. Ask questions about the artwork such as "Why did the artist use these particular colors?" "What message is the artist trying to get across in this

work?" "What can I learn from this piece of art, or how can I connect it to my own life?"

2. Spend time in a natural environment. Whether you visit the beach, park or National forest, try to find ways to experience the wonders that nature has to offer. Private experiences with the natural world are an excellent source of inspiration for many people.

3. Spirituality and inspiration are often directly linked to one another. Pursue spiritual ideas, goals and knowledge. Pray, meditate on spiritual ideas, seek deeper knowledge of a higher power.

4. Read poetry, fiction, essays, drama, and any other pieces of creative literature that interest you. People with strong inspirational intelligence often read classic literature and are drawn to Shakespeare, Poe, Dickens and other creative individuals from the past.

5. Ask questions of life, objects, people, yourself. Only by questioning what is around you or within you, are you likely to find answers.

6. Explore the philosophical writings of the world's most famous thinkers. Endeavor to think like them.

7. Look for quotes or sayings that mean something to you. Ask how you can apply the ideas to your own life.

Ways to Increase Imagination

Imagination is something we all have, but we don't all endeavor to use often enough. Do you see daydreaming as a waste of time? Do you believe that the only productive use of your time is spent in physical activity or activity which requires analytical thinking? If so the first step toward increasing your imaginative intelligence is to change your internal views on the subject.

Some of the most successful individuals are creatively talented people. Imagination is not necessary only to those who work in fields traditionally considered "artistic", however. Regardless of the type of work you do, successfully using your imagination can improve your ability to do your job well.

Whether your imaginative thinking allows you to dream up new inventions or to envision new approaches to familiar problems, by taking an imaginative and creative approach to your position, you are more likely to succeed professionally.

Things to Do

1. Daydream, fantasize, pretend, imagine...

2. Envision new opportunities, products, services or business ideas.

3. Write creatively. Tell a story, write a poem, essay or screenplay.

4. Draw, scribble, make random shapes, lines and other doodles. Create something interesting from whatever emerges.

5. Record the ideas that pop into your mind, regardless of how ridiculous, silly or implausible they appear at first. Imagine ways to make the ideas better.

6. Read books that require you to imagine new ideas, envision new worlds or hypothesize new ideas and situations. Science fiction, fantasy and futuristic novels can be excellent ways to provoke your imaginative intelligence.

How to Increase Innovative Intelligence

Innovation is one of the most necessary components to business success. If you doubt this, try doing a simple internet search of the words "innovate" and "innovative". What you will discover is that innovation virtually spells success in the business world. There are literally thousands of advertisements promoting innovative products, ideas, services and more.

What is so great about innovation? In a nutshell, innovation is creativity brought to life. It represents the cutting edge, the newest, most modern method or approach. The innovative idea is, quite possibly, that creative solution the world has been searching for.

Are you someone who always does things "by the book?" Do you follow the rules, walk in the lines, stick with the "tried and true"? If so, then improving your innovative intelligence could be one of the most crucial factors to your future business success.

Do you...

1. Have a lot of new ideas, but no sense of how to develop them?

2. Let your ideas fade into oblivion, due to a lack of self-confidence or fear

of failure?

3. Have a rigid sense of the "right and wrong" way to do things?

4. Favor traditional methods and approaches over "risky" new ideas?

5. Tend to get stuck in patterns and routines, finding them difficult to break?

6. Choose the known route, as opposed to exploring other options or opportunities?

Everyone has the tendency to get stuck in a rut now and then. Keep in mind, however, that if your business model does not include anything that is new or innovative, the potential for being left behind by those who are thinking ahead will become more and more of a threat as time goes by.

Things to Do

1. Make an effort to stay informed about new ideas, new technology and new approaches to familiar problems.

2. Test new models, theories and approaches. Compare them to the ones you are familiar with. What are the advantages? Disadvantages?

3. Make a solid effort toward bringing one original concept or idea to life.

4. Examine the "tried and true" products or methods which you are used to. Ask "How can I improve on this?"

5. Pick one system or approach that you have been using for a long time and make a point to find another way of doing things.

6. Break your routine. Try doing your morning activities in the evening and your evening activities in the morning.

7. Do things which are out of the ordinary for you.

More Things to Do to Increase Creative Intelligence

At Work

1. Group brainstorming sessions provide an excellent way to get everyone's creative energy flowing. If you do not work in a group setting, use brainstorming techniques on your own. These can involve:

a. Set a goal regarding the number of solutions or ideas you will generate regarding the subject at hand. Make it a point to come up with no less than 20 ideas, whether realistic or absurd.

b. Set a time limit for generating ideas; usually no more than 20 minutes. Write down every idea that comes into your mind in that time, no matter how off the wall it seems.

c. On again, off again brainstorming requires that you write ideas for a given amount of time, then stop for a given amount of time, then start again, until you have either come up with a workable idea, or have exhausted your supply of ideas. This approach generally calls for three minutes of writing, followed by three minutes of reflection and thinking. Try doodling or drawing during the off time, to keep your mind active and engaged.

2. Mind-mapping techniques can be very useful in generating new ideas. Start with a center problem, question or thought. Using arrows or lines going outward, add relevant information, ideas or concepts. Build on each new concept or idea, with more arrows going outward. Include questions, potential problems, or possible benefits, continuing to move outward from the central idea. There are many software programs on the market that provide digital mind-mapping formats. While these can be useful for individuals working on their own, they are less helpful if you will be using mind-mapping as part of a group brainstorming project.

3. Design a creative environment. While traditional work environments are often rather boring, in order to improve creative thinking at work try bringing in color and light, also art, sculpture, interesting furnishings etc...Play background music or nature sounds, water flowing, birds singing etc...While the environment you create should not be distracting, the right blend of these elements can help set the stage for creative work flow.

Outside of Work

1. Play word games. Games that require you to see new words inside existing ones can help increase your ability to look at things in a more creative way.

2. Try out some of the activities at creativitygames.net. This site offers new games and activities weekly, all designed to get your creative energy flowing.

3. Visit artsology.com for unique, hands on art experiences and inspirational resources. Try the geometric artmaker, sandart (version 3) and Abstract Drawing activity (blue field).

4. Any ordinary object can serve as a vehicle to get your creative energy flowing.

Try these activities:

a. Select any random object that is nearby.

b. Try to envision a new use for that object.

c. Make a mental connection between your chosen object and at least 5 other objects that you see. You can make connections based on size, shape, uses, colors or any other ideas that come to mind.

d. Think of at least 5 different ways that the object could be improved upon.

e. Think of 5 different things that you could use instead of, or in place of, that object.

f. Come up with 5 different ideas for things you could combine with that object. How would your new invention function? What would it take to make your new invention real?

By making a point to do these types of activities you are teaching your brain how to see more creatively. As you practice using your mind in new and unusual ways, you will find that the process of creative thinking comes easier than before. You may also have keener intuition, and find that inspirational ideas are more workable, and come much more often. Your innovative intelligence will also increase, as you become used to thinking about how to use familiar objects in new and previously unconnected ways.

Chapter Four
How to Improve Decision-Making Skills

Take a moment to consider how many decisions you make every day. From the moment you wake up in the morning, until the time you fall asleep at night, you are constantly making decisions, both small and large. You decide what to wear, what to eat, when to wake-up, when to fall asleep, whether to read or watch TV, whether to go out or stay in.

Many of our every day decisions are made on a subconscious level. Simply driving a vehicle to and from the store requires that our brains make literally hundreds of split second decisions, from minor steering and speed adjustments to lane changes, turns and stops.

When you approach a red light while driving, you know that it means you should stop. In most instances the decision to stop is made unconsciously. You instinctively slow down, then press on the brake.

Yet, consider those times when you approached a red light and either considered going through it, or did. It is generally not until we are confronted with something out of the ordinary that we consciously think about the decisions that we make.

Knowing that we make hundreds of decisions every day, it stands to reason that our brains are already programmed to quickly and accurately assess situations, formulate a plan for addressing them and finally, to automatically direct our bodies to carry out the actions required to deal with those situations.

Much of this decision-making takes place on a subconscious level. Often, before our conscious minds even realize what happened, our subconscious has already dealt with a situation successfully.

What Happened? Brain Processes Involved in Decision Making

If you have ever been confronted with a life-threatening situation, there is a good chance that you have also looked back and asked "What just happened?" You may be unsure of your own actions, have difficulty remembering what you said or did, and feel as if you can only remember small bits and pieces of the event that you just experienced.

So what did happen? Evidence suggests that the human brain draws from a variety of resources when engaged in the decision making process. Recent studies demonstrate that, while left brain logic and reasoning centers are used somewhat during the decision making process, the brain also relies on a number of other important functions to facilitate this process.

1. Sensory Input Centers: The first step in the decision making process is "information gathering". The brain employs those areas which control sensory input to gather information about the situation. Experiments on both humans and animals demonstrate that visual, auditory and olfactory centers of the brain are highly active during this initial phase of the decision making process.

2. Memory Centers: Brain wave patterns of test subjects show that those areas of the brain which store and replay memory are triggered into action when the subject is asked to make a decision. The brain draws on its core knowledge of similar events and situations, to decide how to respond to the current situation.

3. Creativity Centers: Surprisingly the brain also draws on its creative centers, presumably to hypothesize new courses of action. Studies in laboratory rats suggest that the animals attempt to simulate unknown situations and events, when engaged in the decision making process.

4. Object processing and reasoning centers are activated, as the brain draws conclusions about the situation and decides on a course of action.

5. Left Brain, Logic Centers: While the final resolution to the situation may be generated in the areas of the brain which have previously been known to handle logical thought, little is known about how the information is shared from one region of the brain to the next, and no-one is absolutely certain how the final decision is reached.

As we consider what processes the brain goes through to make just a single decision, we must also keep in mind that in many cases these processes occur on a subconscious level, and in a split-second of time.

Since our subconscious minds are unimaginably intelligent, and amazingly well equipped for making decisions, why is that some of us have trouble with this process?

Subconscious versus Conscious

The conscious and subconscious minds work together most of the time, without our truly being aware of it. The "sudden thoughts" we often randomly experience, the quick flashes of memory, the great ideas that hit us, seemingly out of nowhere, the little urges, cravings, and unexplained feelings...these are all evidence that our mind operates on more than one level.

On the one hand, our conscious mind is usually preoccupied with whatever task is at hand, preparing for a business meeting, discussing ideas for a fund-raiser, even cooking dinner or simply watching TV.

On the other hand, however, regardless of what we are doing consciously, our subconscious mind is processing a realm of other information. It may be absorbing details about our surroundings, working on a problem we have been consciously struggling with or even assessing our overall condition and gathering information on our general health and well-being.

We are constantly receiving messages and signals from our subconscious mind, every day. When you have been working long and hard on a project, then suddenly find that you are craving a cup of coffee so much that you can almost smell it, taste it, this is a message from your subconscious, telling you it's time to take a break.

Often the subconscious works most successfully when the conscious mind is less active. For example, you are watching a TV show and suddenly remember where you left that important document - which you thought you had lost altogether. Or, you are just about to fall asleep, when you suddenly remember that you forgot to turn off the oven. Only after your conscious mind was "turned off" was your subconscious able to convey these important messages and insights.

While the subconscious most often operates below the surface of conscious thought, it also can shut off or bypass your conscious mind, when necessary. This most often happens in cases where there is great emotional trauma or the risk of physical danger is imminent. In these cases the subconscious, which is able to operate much faster and more efficiently than the conscious mind, will literally take over the situation.

Conscious decision making is often a difficult undertaking, only because our conscious mind gets in the way. Imagine that you are in a life or death situation and you needed to make a decision about how to respond. Do you make a decision tree, or diagram the situation and all of its possible outcomes? Do you hem and haw or second guess yourself? Do you select a course of action and then change your mind eight times? If you approached a life or death situation in any of those ways, you would never survive the impending disaster.

Your subconscious takes over in situations like these because it inherently knows what to do. The main question then, seems to be that if your subconscious can gather information, process it, compare it to what is already known, simulate it hypothetically with what is not known and draw a conclusion, all in a matter of just a few seconds, why is it so difficult to make decisions on a conscious level?

What Factors Inhibit Decision Making?

Undeniably, the biggest factor that can inhibit or impair a person's ability to make decisions is self. Lack of self-confidence, fear of failure, and even fear of the unknown are all possible causes of difficulty, when it comes to making decision.

Factors that affect decision making which are directly related to areas of intelligence could include: visual and sensory intelligence, abstract thinking skills, logical thinking skills, verbal and communication skills, and memory and recall abilities.

A study which was published in Science Daily magazine also suggests that people of different IQ levels may approach the decision making process in different ways. This study shows that the order in which the various brain functions are employed to reach a conclusion can be different in people with higher and lower IQ scores.

How to Increase Intelligence in Areas Involved with the Decision Making Process

Possibly the most important step you can take to improve your decision making abilities is to embark on a quest to increase your introspective intelligence skills. Because many of the factors that influence decision making include inherent personality traits such as lack of self-confidence, fear of failure and fear of change, increasing intelligence in areas such as self awareness and self discovery, can be very helpful in helping you make decisions with clarity and self-assurance.

In "*The Psychology of Intelligence and Will*", HG Wyatt speculates that the nature of intelligence and higher thought processes may only be able to be understood through introspective methods, rather than external means, such as tests, experiments and so forth. He defines introspection as the doorway for "conscious to subconscious" communication. Meaning, when we are seeking answers about ourselves, from ourselves, we open a new doorway which allows our conscious and subconscious minds to communicate more readily.

Introspective Intelligence can be increased in a number of ways, including:

1. Meditation

2. Quiet reflection

3. Journaling

4. Creative writing

5. Art

Introspection is most often facilitated by a quiet room or outdoor setting, and a solitary environment. You may also wish to explore guided introspection activities, such as those led by a therapist, counselor or other professional.

When we are using our introspective intelligence, we are exploring our own conscious and subconscious minds and seeking answers about ourselves; our thoughts, actions, feelings and behaviors. Often times when we look within ourselves, we find our subconscious has answers which we were not aware of, before that time.

You will not improve introspective intelligence by simply doing these things on occasion, or at sporadic intervals, when you think you need to. However, by participating regularly in introspective activities, writing, journaling, meditation and so on, you can strengthen your intelligence in this area. Increased introspective intelligence and better communication with the subconscious mind allows for better decision making abilities. By understanding your own inner thought process, you can rid yourself of the fears or doubts that may stand in the way of your ability to make decisions easily. You will build a greater sense of trust in your own abilities, and you will learn how to make decisions on an intuitive level, rather than an entirely logical one.

Getting Information from the Subconscious to the Conscious Mind

The University of Pittsburgh, Learning Research and Development Center published findings gathered from a number of research projects during a ten year period. The published paper "Cognitive-Skill Acquisition" was written by "Kurt Van Lehn" and published in "Annual Psychology Review."

The purpose of the studies which were reviewed was to determine whether it was possible for adult subjects to gain new cognitive skills, as well as to identify the best methods for gaining those skills. The term "cognitive skills" refers to the ability to solve intellectual problems and carry out tasks involving "higher" thought processes.

The most notable finding was that cognitive skills, like many other skills, can be acquired through regular practice. The author compares the process of gaining new cognitive skills to that of learning to drive a car.

When we first get behind the wheel of a car, we are both unfamiliar and uncomfortable with the many processes involved in driving. As we practice and become more comfortable with driving, however, the processes become like second nature to us. After a few years of driving, we no longer have to consciously think about every detail. We instinctively know where the brake is, how far to turn the wheel, how much gas we need to achieve a certain speed and how to perform all the other tasks, which we were once unsure of.

By rehearsing cognitive processes we can "train" our subconscious to handle complex problems or tackle difficult tasks in the same way. We have all heard the saying "practice makes perfect." People learn many skills over the course of a lifetime, from playing an instrument to knitting a sweater, with practice and repetition these tasks are soon performed without conscious thought.

Applying this knowledge to improve your decision making skills involves first becoming familiar with the processes involved in decision making, and then practicing those processes on a conscious level, daily.

How Do You Make Decisions?

Whether or not you are aware of it, you already have an established process for making decisions.

Let's look at a simple decision that you most likely made at least once today. What to eat. When you made that decision last, which of the following did you do...

1. Did you check the kitchen to see what was available?

For such a seemingly simple task, you employed many cognitive skills. You used visual and sensory intelligence, as well as object recognition skills. You also used memory, to recall information about each item you encountered i.e. how it tastes, smells, looks, whether you like it or dislike it, how difficult it is to prepare, and what other items can be prepared with it.

2. Did you formulate one or more possible plans, based on the information that you gathered?

For this step you also employed several decision making skills. You drew on memory to some extent whether remembering how to make your favorite meatloaf or recalling how it smells when it's cooking or how good it tastes when you eat it. You demonstrated advanced logic and deductive reasoning skills, simply by looking through the items and deciding which you could use and which you could not. Finally, in this phase you relied on pattern recognition abilities, and you may have unknowingly grouped items together, Italian ingredients, Asian ingredients, Mexican and American etc... You demonstrated your ability to identify "what goes where".

3. Did you look for flaws in one or more of your plans?

If you decided not to make meatloaf because you realized there was only one egg left in the carton, then you looked for and identified flaws in your plan.

4. Did you arrive at a final decision and carry out your plan?

If so you have already demonstrated that you are capable of making and implementing logical decisions. You have also demonstrated the ability to intelligently use a wide range of thought processes.

When considering this example of decision making, it is important to keep in mind that most often we are not aware of the processes our brain employs when making minor every day decisions. Yet, even though we are not aware, our brain is still carrying out many complex tasks, often quickly and without difficulty.

Simplifying the Decision Making Process

The process of making sound decisions is the same, regardless of whether you need to make a major or minor decision. You can approach a complex decision in the same way that you approach a decision about where to eat or which movie to see this weekend.

1. Gather information

2. Evaluate the information against known and unknown variables.

3. Formulate one or more plans of action.

4. Look for flaws in the plan.

5. Make a decision and implement the desired plan.

By consciously playing out these steps daily with each decision that you are faced with, your conscious mind will become more familiar with the decision making process. You will soon become more willing to trust the subconscious mind's ability to handle decisions, even those made in a work environment.

By working to bring subconscious processes to the forefront, you will find that you are increasing communication between the conscious and subconscious minds. You will also find that decision making begins to come easier and faster than before. By allowing your conscious mind to actively participate in previously subconscious processes, you open the door to allowing the subconscious to teach the conscious mind how to make better decisions.

Additional Things to Do to Improve Decision Making Abilities

1. Hone your observation skills

a. Use peripheral vision to observe your surroundings. Take mental notes of what you notice.

b. Try to remember all the items in a specific location on your desk at work, on your bedside table at home, or in the console of your car.

c. Exercise your powers of observation by playing computer or game system games that require you to search for and locate items, to remember the locations of specific items or to observe minute details, to solve a puzzle or complete a sequence.

2. Improve sequencing and patterning skills

a. Look for patterns or similarities among seemingly unrelated items.

b. Play games that require you to spot the differences between two objects, or to decide what two or more objects have in common.

c. Play matching games that require you to work quickly to locate all items that are the same or different.

3. Improve creative thinking skills

a. Make a point to expose yourself to something new every day. Whether you try a new food, visit a new place or read something out of the ordinary for you, opening your mind to new experiences is a good way to improve creative thinking.

b. Hypothesize unrealistic solutions to realistic problems. Make a point to think "out of the box".

c. Listen to music, visit art museums, read or write poetry, expose yourself to the creativity of others.

Quick Insight Activity

Imagine that you have two minds, and that both can operate at the same time. If it helps, try imagining yourself with two heads. Give each of your two brains a different name.

Write a short story about what it is like to have two functioning brains. No-one else will see your work, so don't worry about how dumb it sounds, or how bad your spelling might be.

When writing your story, answer each question:

1. What skills does each one of your two brains handle?

2. How do your two brains get along with one another?

3. Do your two minds communicate well? What methods of communication do they have?

4. What are the problems and the benefits of having two different brains?

5. What messages do your two minds have for one another?

6. Is one brain more in control than the other?

Once you have written your story, take a few moments to look back and reflect. Hopefully, this exercise will provide you with new insights into yourself, as well as your conscious and subconscious thought processes.

Chapter Five
How to Solve Problems Quickly and Effectively

Problem solving skills are directly related to both professional success and success in other areas of life. Whether you need to be able to quickly fix problems that arise on an assembly line or simply identify the reason why your car has stalled out on the highway, the more effectively you are able to deal with personal and professional challenges, the more productive you will be in life.

Types of Problems

A problem is anything that interferes with your ability to obtain a current goal. While many types of problems can arise in every day work and life situations, most can be placed into the following groups:

External concrete: External problems are problems that occur in the world outside of ourselves. External problems generally require a physical solution. When something breaks, a piece doesn't fit correctly or some other physical reality interferes with our desire to accomplish a given task, the problem falls into this category.

External abstract: External abstract problems also occur outside of ourselves, but this type of problem most commonly requires a mental solution. Mathematical equations, scientific formulas and other types of analytical problems fall into this category. While most external abstract problems have a solution which can be applied to the physical world, the process involved in finding that solution generally requires a mathematical or scientific approach.

Internal concrete: Physical disabilities, illness and other physical health related problems that interfere with our ability to meet certain goals, can be thought to be internal, concrete problems.

Internal abstract: These types of problems are emotionally based. The solutions to these types of problems are often found through introspection and increased self awareness. Internal abstract problems may include negative attitudes, mistaken beliefs, conflicting emotions and other abstract thoughts or ideas, which interfere with our ability to be successful either at work or in our personal lives.

Solving Problems

Problem solving and decision making abilities are closely linked to one another. Being able to effectively make decisions is instrumental to problem solving, since it requires the ability to choose the most appropriate solution and formulate a plan for implementing that solution. The opposite is also true, however, since the ability to identify and solve problems is instrumental to the decision making process as well.

Gathering Information

Regardless of the type of problem you need to solve, the first step is to gather as much information about the problem as possible, in the shortest amount of time. This process is similar to the process described in the decision making chapter of this book.

Consider this hypothetical situation: You are the general manager at a manufacturing plant. One of your assembly lines has suddenly stopped production.

The first thing you need to do is assess the situation. While the main problem is that the production line has become inoperable, you need to find out as much information about the problem as possible, before you can formulate a solution.

The information gathering process includes asking questions and looking for answers, to gain a better perspective of the problem.

Questions:

What?

Where?

Why?

How?

When?

How long?

Example: In the hypothetical situation, the questions you ask might look like this:

a. What? What is keeping the assembly line from operating properly?

b. Where? Where on the line is the problem originating?

c. Why? Why is the equipment not functioning properly?

d. How? What happened? Did a machine jam? Was the equipment used improperly?

e. When? When did the problem first occur?

f. How long has the problem been occurring?

All of these questions are important. Finding the answers will help you gain a better perspective of the problem, giving you the ability to determine the most effective possible solutions.

In our hypothetical situation, after asking these questions you were able to determine that a broken conveyor belt is responsible for the problem.

Clarifying Goals

The next step in the problem solving process is to think about your goals and determine how the problem is affecting your ability to meet those goals.

Define your goal by asking: What am I trying to accomplish?

Hypothetical Example: Make 2700 parts by 5:00.

Effective problem solving often involves redefining, restating and clarifying goals by examining them from several perspectives. Consider both long and short term objectives, as well as the most immediate goals that need to be met.

Original hypothetical statement of goal: Make 2700 parts by 5:00.

Your revised goals might also include:

1. Get the production line up and running again. (short term)

2. Repair the conveyor belt. (short term)

3. Determine what is wrong with the conveyor belt. (immediate)

4. Make 10,000 parts before Friday (long term)

Each of these statements clarifies what you are trying to accomplish. Some of the statements address your immediate goals, while others look at the situation from an extended point of view. Looking at the goal or objective from several different viewpoints can help you clarify the problem, so that you can begin to formulate possible solutions.

Identifying the Problem

Use the information you have gathered to determine what is interfering with your ability to meet your goals and objectives. To get the best perspective on the problem consider both the original and redefined goals.

Ask:

What? What is stopping me from meeting this goal?

What else?

How? In what ways is this problem preventing me from accomplishing what I need to?

Why? Why is this problem keeping me from meeting my goals?

Hypothetical example: Original goal: Make 2700 parts before 5:00.

By asking "what", you first state the obvious

"A broken conveyor belt is stopping me from meeting this goal".

By looking closer at the problem, and asking questions such as "what else?", "how" and "why", you will get a better perspective of the problem, and will be able to identify a greater range of potential solutions.

Continuing with the example:

a. A broken conveyor belt. (What else? "How" and "Why"?)

b. No-one available to do repairs to the conveyor belt.

c. Halted assembly line.

d. Time wasted.

e. Idle workers.

f. Falling behind in production schedule.

When defining the problem make sure that you keep referring back to the goal. Repeat this process with each redefined goal.

Now instead of having one narrowly defined problem, with only one potential solution, you have a longer list of clearly defined problems. This allows you to identify and implement a greater number of solutions.

Brainstorming Solutions

Once you have clarified the problems, the next step is to determine ways to solve them. Extend the focus of your problem solving to each problem identified in the previous step.

Brainstorming involves asking and answering questions about the problem. Successful problem-solving depends not only on your ability to find solutions to problems, but may also depend on your ability to identify ways to meet your goals in spite of the problem.

Some questions to ask during brainstorming might include:

a. How can I work around the problem?

b. How can I lessen the impact of the problem?

c. How can I work with the problem?

Being able to view the problem in several ways provides you with better opportunities to work out a solution, or several solutions, to get back on track toward meeting your goals.

Examples:

Problem: Halted assembly Line

Questions:

How can I get the assembly line running again?

How can I operate the assembly line without the conveyor belt?

How can the parts be made without the assembly line?

Possible Solutions:

1. Call in an outside repair person to get the assembly line running again.

2. Have workers do the work normally done by the conveyor belt.

3. Keep the parts of the assembly line that are working properly going, stopping production at the broken conveyor belt.

4. Substitute another piece of equipment in place of the broken one.

5. Make parts manually.

To solve problems effectively, keep reviewing and clarifying goals, asking questions and brainstorming solutions, until you have found one, or several, that will get you back on track toward meeting your defined goals.

Improving Reaction Time - Speed Thinking Basics

In many cases problem solving must be done quickly, sometimes in a matter of only minutes. In a work situation, the faster you can effectively solve a problem the more productive you will be.

The concept of speed thinking was first conceived in the 1970s, and many have since expounded on the idea. The principle idea behind the concept of speed thinking is that many people work best in high pressure situations. It was hypothesized that by limiting the amount of time available for problem solving, most people will find an effective solution to a given problem within the designated time.

Overview of Accelerated Problem Solving

Using accelerated thinking techniques you can solve most problems within a time span of three to five minutes. To use this approach you must be familiar with the basic techniques applied in problem-solving and be prepared to streamline your own thought process.

The technique requires you to move quickly through each step in the problem solving process. You are required to set time limits for each phase and stick to those limits.

1. Information gathering phase:
    a. Identify the problem
    b. Identify the causes or possible causes of the problem
2. Processing/Organizing/Formulating phase
    a. Questioning
    b. Clarifying
    c. Redefining
3. Brainstorming
    What are all the possible solutions?
4. Planning for Implementation of Solutions
    a. How?
    b. Who?
    c. When?
    d. Where?
    e. To what extent?

To move quickly through the steps, it is best to set a time limit of 60 to 90 seconds per phase. When one phase is completed, move to the next phase.

Considerations

Regardless of whether you are attempting to solve a problem using the speed thinking method or more traditional methods, failure to quickly and effectively solve a problem usually results from one of the following:

Information Gathering Phase

1. Missing information: Are you certain you have all the information necessary to obtain a workable solution to your problem?

2. Misinterpreted information: When gathering information always make a point to clarify what you heard, saw or read about the problem. Double check information, to make sure it is accurate.

3. Assumed information: Many times when we approach a problem we assume information about one or more ideas pertaining to it. If our assumptions are incorrect, any solution we arrive at is likely to be ineffective.

Processing/Formulating/Redefining Phase

1. Poorly defining the problem

2. Misinterpreting the problem

3. False assumptions about the problem

The more familiar we are with a given situation, the more likely we may be to assume we already know what the problem is and how we can solve it. While applying practical knowledge and experience in this way can work in many situations, in some situations our preconceived ideas interfere with our ability to find an effective solution.

Brainstorming Phase

1. Assuming the first solution is correct

2. Narrowing options for possible solutions

3. Ruling out possible solutions based on assumptions

Planning and Implementation Phase

1. Overlooking one or more steps necessary to implementation

2. Overstating the importance of a single part of the process, i.e. identifying what will be done, but not who, how or when.

3. Assuming information about one or more parts of the implementation

process, i.e. "It normally takes 3 days to receive an order" or "it usually takes me an hour to make all my calls".

When working on a plan for implementation of a solution, consider all aspects of the process as well as any possible variables which may arise during the implementation process.

Other Things to Do to Improve Problem solving Skills

At Work

1. Experiment with different problem solving methods.

2. Memorize the steps to effective problem solving and practice applying them in a variety of situations.

3. Use visual aids for problem solving.

4. Hold group sessions and implement a speed thinking technique for problem solving.

Outside of Work

1. Put together 3-D puzzles.

2. Solve the nine dots problem.

3. Try building your own robots or experimenting with simple robotics.

4. Work through complex mathematical problems.

5. Visit playwithyourmind.com. Check out Tripples, Pochle, Circular Logic and other games designed to improve your problem solving skills (free games, with no download required).

6. Explore scientific ideas. Make an effort to identify the theories and principles that govern everyday situations, products or events.

7. Explore lateral thinking problems.

Chapter Six
How to Concentrate Deeply and Avoid Distractions

Concentration is the mind's ability to focus on a given task. The amount of time which we are able to focus on any one task is what is known as the attention span. Being able to pay close attention to the task you are attending to, as well as being able to remain focused on a task until it is completed, are both crucial elements for overall success in most work situations.

Understanding your work habits and becoming more familiar with your individual attention span, is often the first step toward improving concentration. While individual attention spans can range from as little as twenty minutes all the way up to as much as ninety minutes, the average person has an attention span of about 50 minutes.

Test Yourself

To determine your current attention span, begin by doing the following activity.

1. Set aside a two hour time span. Make sure to schedule this activity to take place during the time of day when you feel you are the most productive.

2. Set your mind to a task that you are comfortable with. A research project, a school or work assignment or some other task which will require you to focus deeply for a long time.

3. Work in an environment where there are limited distractions. Turn off background noise, such as television and radio. Ask others to not disturb you during this time.

4. Before starting to work on your chosen task, place a pen and a piece of paper near you.

5. Write down the time you begin working on the project.

6. Note the time when you first notice your mind straying from the task at hand. Next to the time, write down a single word describing the interrupting thought.

7. Bring yourself back to the task, by refocusing your thoughts and directing yourself to complete the project.

8. Note the time of the second incident, in which you notice your mind

wandering from the task. Refocus and approach the project again.

9. Keep repeating this process until you have reached the point where you feel you can no longer refocus your mind on the given task, without taking a break.

Questions to Consider

A. How long were you able to work from the beginning of the experiment to the end? Total time (in minutes) _________

B. How far into the project were you before your mind first drifted to something else? Total time (in minutes) _________

C. How many times did your mind drift during the project?

Number of times__________

D. How difficult was it for you to refocus your thoughts after your mind first wandered from the task?

Rate the difficulty on a scale from one to five. On this scale, one represents minimal to no difficulty and five represents extreme difficulty.

1 2 3 4 5

E. Did the quality of your work diminish from beginning to end? Yes No

F. What thoughts interrupted your concentration? Do the same thoughts occur several times?

G. How long were you able to work in between each refocusing point?

Longest period of time (in minutes)_____________

Shortest period of time (in minutes)____________

As you consider the information which you have discovered from this activity, keep in mind that it can be applied to help you improve concentration and increase attention span.

Developing a Personal Plan for Increasing Attention Span

Use the information from the personal assessment to formulate a plan for increasing your attention span.

Decreasing Intrusive Thoughts

Once you have identified the thoughts which are interrupting your concentration, develop a plan to deal with them. Some of the most common interruptions in thought process are unattended basic personal needs. Others stem from outside stressors; relationship problems, financial concerns, work overload and other work and life difficulties can cause your mind to wander from the task at hand.

To minimize the number of times your thoughts stray from the current project, try the following:

1. Attend to basic personal needs before starting to work on a project. Eat a light snack or meal before starting work. Don't keep beverages close by, especially if they encourage you to change your focus. Instead, choose to drink beverages only on scheduled breaks. Also, use the bathroom before starting your project and again at break times. Deal with climate control issues ahead of time as well. Adjust the room temperature or keep a jacket or sweater nearby, when conditions make it necessary to do so.

2. Deal with outside stressors before taking on a big project. Don't put off dealing with an angry boss or coworker, for example, until after you have completed work. This will only make it harder for you to focus on the task at hand.

3. Schedule work times for the hours of the day when you are likely to be at your personal best. If you are a morning person, for instance, make it a point to work on the most difficult tasks during this time, approaching less difficult tasks in the afternoon or evening. Whenever possible, do not choose times when you are angry, stressed out or worried about something to start on a difficult assignment.

4. Set aside a specific time every day that is just for worrying and thinking. While this is not a technique that most people would consider, knowing that you have a designated time for worrying, thinking and even daydreaming, can help keep your mind on task when you need it to be. It can also make refocusing your thoughts easier, since you can simply remind yourself "At six o'clock I will worry about that. Right now I will stay focused on what I'm doing."

5. Don't try not to think about a certain issue or topic that is affecting your train of thought. Trying not to think of something generally makes us think about it even more. Instead, acknowledge the thought, write it down, if necessary, and then (similar to the idea presented in item 4) schedule a specific time for thinking about, worrying about or otherwise dealing with it.

6. Balance your workload. When you feel overextended, you are more likely to be distracted by thoughts like "I have to get this done by 5:00" or "I have to get started on my next assignment soon." Procrastinating and taking on more work than you are able to handle are two main causes of this. When you are stressed over the amount of work you have to get done or are worried that you don't have enough time to complete your work, you will find that you are more distracted than when you give yourself an appropriate amount of time to complete the tasks you need to finish.

Increasing Attention Span

For the next two weeks plan to spend no longer than the total time (question one) found on your personal assessment, working on any one task or assignment. If you need to work for a longer time, schedule breaks of at least 15 minutes. Optionally, if you are unable to take breaks at work, shift your focus from one task to another, spending no more than the given amount of time on any one project.

After two weeks, plan to increase the total amount of time which you spend working on one task by five minutes. Work in the same manner described previously, scheduling breaks or alternating tasks for another two weeks.

Continue to increase the time by five minutes, every two weeks, until you have reached the point where increasing it again is not feasible for you.

Medical Conditions Associated with Difficulty Concentrating

In some cases difficulty concentrating can be caused by an underlying medical condition. ADD and ADHD are two common causes of an inability to focus, or to stay focused on tasks which require mental concentration. Both adults and children can be affected by ADD or ADHD, but in most cases the condition is diagnosed either in childhood or adolescence.

Insomnia and other sleep conditions can affect concentration levels as well. Irregular sleep patterns or failure to enter the REM sleep state can result in a significant decrease in normal mental performance.

Hyperthyroidism affects approximately three to five percent of the population in the U.S. This condition, which interferes with the normal production of hormones associated with healthy brain function, can impair focus and concentration abilities, and may also contribute to a lack of clarity in thought.

Depression, anxiety and other mental health conditions can also cause a decrease in your ability to focus and concentrate. Conditions such as Post Traumatic Stress Disorder and other traumatic stress related conditions are known to interfere with concentration.

Nutritional imbalances or deficiencies can have a direct impact on brain function. Additionally, the consumption of certain processed and refined foods has been shown to interfere with cognitive abilities, and may have an immediate, temporary impact on mental performance. The last chapter of this book gives detailed information on diet and nutrition, as it relates to brain health.

All the above conditions can be easily treated, once they have been identified by a medical professional. If you have experienced a noticeable decline in mental performance, it may be beneficial to talk to a doctor or other medical expert.

Other Things to Do

While there has not been a great deal of research regarding successful techniques for improving concentration and focus, recent studies indicate that the "dual n-back task" has been able to improve memory, concentration and focus. Participants in these early experiments have demonstrated improved cognitive test scores, after six weeks of daily training with the dual n- back task.

A free on line version of the dual n-back task can be found at dualn-back.com. Composed of both visual and auditory stimuli, the dual n-back task requires participants to identify previous stimuli, under progressively more difficult circumstances. To gain optimal results, it is recommended that you work with the program for at least 25 minutes per day.

❖   ❖   ❖

Chapter Seven
How to Improve Memory and Recall Abilities

Many people commonly relate intelligence to the ability to recall information and recite facts. While memory and recall abilities do not necessarily define intelligence, they certainly do play a large part in determining overall success, in a variety of work environments.

As discussed in earlier chapters of this book, the subconscious mind stores all the information which we are exposed to, every moment of every day. If this is true, then we never really forget anything. When we say we "can't remember something", the real problem lies in our inability to access the information when we need or want to recall it.

Difficulties in recalling important information can present a great deal of difficulty in the workplace. Have you ever…

1. Walked out of the house without an important document, even though you reminded yourself over and over not to forget it?

2. Been in the middle of working on an important project, but suddenly found you could not recall some of the major details you needed to include?

3. Had to stop what you were doing to look something up, simply because you could not remember the information?

4. Missed an important meeting or deadline, because you simply forgot it?

5. Forgot where you put a piece of equipment, tool or some other item you were just working with?

These types of situations are typical of the many ways that an ability to recall information can slow down or halt productivity on the job.

Why We Forget

Since our brains are always filtering and storing information in order of perceived relevance, it stands to reason that not everything we see, hear, sense, or otherwise become exposed to, is available for immediate recall. Unless you have a photographic memory, many details of your everyday work and life experiences will be stored out of reach of the conscious mind. When our brain works the way we want it to, however, important information is immediately available for access.

The main reason for an inability to recall certain information, therefore, is that the brain has placed that information out of reach of the conscious mind. In most cases this is because the subconscious has decided that the information is not necessary to our ability to function on a daily basis. The brain may also filter the information downward simply because we are focusing on some other important task at the moment.

Memory and Stress

Stress can have a great impact on our ability to remember. When we have a large number of tasks to complete or when a task we are working on is pushing us to the limits of personal ability, the brain is more likely to filter information which it views as being unrelated to the immediate stressors, downward. This is why there are times when we can recall seemingly minor details about one thing, but not the major facts regarding something else.

When the mind perceives itself as being overloaded or over burdened with details, there is also a greater chance that important information will not be processed in the same way that it would be if we were relaxed, calm and feeling in control. This can happen when events occur in rapid succession or when we are asked to grasp a large amount of information in a very short time. This type of "rapid-fire input" causes the brain to sort information on a different level of awareness, often resulting in portions of the information being stored outside of our immediate recall ability.

Because stress is often directly related to an inability to recall important information, decreasing the amount of stress that you feel both at work and at home, is often a successful method of improving memory and recall ability. Chapter Eight of this book addresses stress in greater detail, and provides helpful suggestions on ways to manage the impact of stress in the workplace.

Memory and Focus

A second major factor related to how our brain processes and stores information is focus. When we are concentrating solely on a certain subject, the information which we are exposed to is more likely to be stored at a level that is accessible to the conscious mind. On the contrary, if the information is presented to us when we are concentrating on another, unrelated task, the brain is more likely to filter the information away from the conscious mind. By doing this, the subconscious is allowing us to focus on whatever task we are trying to complete at the moment.

If you have difficulty focusing on information or paying attention for long periods of time, Chapter Six provides helpful information on improving concentration and focus.

General Tips for Improving Recall Abilities

1. Make an effort to focus on the given information for at least 30 seconds.

2. If the information is visual, take a mental picture of it.

3. Put the information together in an uncommon way. For example make up a rhyme, song or poem, or use alliterative terms to help you remember. For example "Polly's payroll needs perfecting" might help you remember to look for errors in an employee's wages.

4. Plaster names on faces. If you have trouble recalling names, try imagining the name written in bold colors and plastered across the person's body or face. Also associating the person's name with a description, such as "Silly Sue" or "Jolly John" may help you remember more clearly.

5. Draw pictures that will help you link the information together. Some people choose to create one large picture, and incorporate all the information they need to remember with symbols or images. Others choose to draw several pictures, then create a scenario which links them together mentally. Whichever method you choose, this common pneumonic technique can help you recall important information when you need it.

6. Write down things you need to recall. The act of writing something down forces you to focus on the information long enough to record it. This simple technique can also help you visualize the information later.

7. Talk to yourself. While some people remember things visually, others remember better when the information is audible. Speaking out loud provides a secondary sensory experience. As another option, if the information is presented to you verbally, try to remember the sound of the presenter's voice, including tone, rhythm, inflection and accent. This experience may help you recall the information, if you are an auditory learner.

Things to Do

Activities to Help Increase Memory

1. Visit improvememory.org to try a number of games which can increase

your ability to remember and recall information.

2. Play games such as "Simon" and "Concentration" on a regular basis. You can also test long term memory skills with trivia and knowledge games, available in both on and off-line versions.

3. Exercise daily. Exercise has been linked to improved brain function and better recall ability. Exercise also helps reduce stress and improve sleep patterns, which may also have a beneficial impact on your ability to concentrate and allow you to focus on specific tasks for greater periods of time.

4. Take a <u>self-test</u> designed to measure both verbal and visual memory. Work to better your score.

5. Test a variety of pneumonic devices to determine which ones are the most helpful for your individual situation.

6. Make simple dietary changes. Eat healthy foods which contain a wide variety of nutrients beneficial to healthy brain function. Avoid processed foods and foods high in sugar and artificial sweeteners.

7. Get an ample amount of sleep. One of the most common causes of temporary memory impairment is fatigue.

8. Break up large tasks. Even after a good night's sleep, attempting to do too much mental work at one time can create "brain fog" i.e. trouble concentrating, thinking clearly or remembering. The brain is a muscle. If you overuse your arms, you expect that the muscles will become tired and work less efficiently. The same concept can be applied to mental work, too much at once will decrease the brain's ability to function at peak levels.

9. If you believe that memory loss is affecting your everyday life, or interfering with your ability to effectively meet work demands, consider consulting a physician.

Chapter Eight
How to Think Clearly Under Stress

Stress can have a major impact on mental performance. It can interfere with your ability to think clearly, make sound decisions and function at peak performance levels. This chapter will briefly discuss the subject of stress, and identify ways to reduce the impact it can have on both body and mind.

Stress in the workplace can be caused by an infinite number of situations. Difficult coworkers, unpleasant bosses or supervisors, too many burdens and responsibilities, working in a field that isn't rewarding, whether mentally or financially and many other factors, can contribute to the presence of stress in a work environment.

While some stress can be a normal part of everyday work and life, excess stress can take a toll on physical, emotional and mental health and well-being. Learning how to think calmly and clearly, even when faced with a great deal of stress and external pressure, can help you be more successful in almost every aspect of life.

Understanding the Brain's Reaction to Stress

Stressful situations can cause the brain to go into what professionals refer to as "survival mode." When this occurs, the 'thinking' or rational part of the brain may have difficulty functioning. On the one hand, we may feel confused, have trouble focusing and have difficulty making decisions or solving problems. On the other hand, very stressful situations can also cause us to react without thinking. Rather than taking the time to make a deliberate and well planned decision, we may jump into action without considering the situation beforehand.

Both unclear thinking and reflex-type reactions can be typical of people who work in very high stress environments. When these types of situations arise, the brain is most likely functioning in survival mode. In the first scenario, the brain goes into "freeze mode". Similar to a deer trapped in a car's headlights, we feel we can't make a decision, regardless of how much effort we put in to trying. In the second scenario, however, the "fight or flight" instinct is triggered. In this case we may fly into action, making snap decisions and hurried judgment calls, before we even realize what we are doing.

Fire fighters, paramedics, rescue workers, emergency room technicians and others who daily work in high stress environments must learn how to manage these reactions, to remain clear headed and able to perform job duties in the most effective manner. Yet office workers, factory workers, sales representatives and stock brokers may also need to learn new ways to handle stress in the workplace.

About Stress

Stress arises when everyday work and life situations cause us to feel threatened in some way. The greater our brain perceives the threat to be, the more likely we are to experience the symptoms of stress.

Obviously we become stressed when our physical well-being is threatened. When we are asked to perform job duties that we feel are unsafe, when accidents or emergency situations arise, or when we sense hostility from others around us. Whether the danger is real or perceived, the brain's response is often the same.

Stress does not occur only when we there is a threat to our physical well-being, however. When we believe that there is a threat to our well-being, such as to our stability, security, happiness or our feeling of success, we may find that we experience the same types of reactions. This type of stress occurs in almost every work environment.

Identifying and Assessing Stress in the Workplace

The best way to deal with stress in the workplace is to learn to identify it's cause. The next time you feel stressed out on the job, keep in mind that there is most likely something about the situation which is causing you to feel threatened.

In many cases the stress we feel is directly related to our perception of the situation:

"I could lose my job over this."

"I can never keep up with all of this work."

"This job is killing me."

"My wife is going to divorce me if I have to keep working late."

Once you have identified the cause of the stress, the next step is to assess the reality of the situation. How likely is it that you will lose your job over the situation? Is it realistic to believe that your wife will leave you if you work late?

Try to rate the threat on a scale of one to ten, with one being least likely to happen and ten being almost a certainty. In most cases, once you have assessed your perception of the situation, you will realize that the threat is not as realistic as you previously felt it was.

Plan for the Worst

If you are faced with the worst possible case scenario, for example if you lose your job, have to take a pay cut or are demoted to a lesser position, will you still manage to survive? How?

Knowing that you have a back-up plan in place, just in case the worst really does happen, is another good way to lessen the amount of stress you feel at work. Keep in mind that life goes on. There may be other, better opportunities available.

Simple Techniques for Thinking Clearly Under Pressure

1. Remain in the moment.

A stressful event can often cause us to call to mind similar events or situations, from the past. If you find yourself thinking "This reminds of …" or saying "The last time this happened…" you are recalling events from the past, which may or may not have any real association with the current situation. While this type of reaction to stress is quite common, if you make an effort to remain in the moment, the current situation will seem less frustrating and you may have an easier time dealing with what is happening right now.

To remain in the moment, if you notice yourself making references to other situations, times or people, take a second to consciously look around you. Notice your surroundings. Reach out and physically touch something that is near you. A desk, chair or any other object close enough to touch can serve as a tool for bringing your thoughts back into focus. This technique, called "grounding" can help you regain control of the moment, when you are in a high stress situation.

2. Prepare for possible high-stress situations.

Train your mind to rely on methods, formulas and standard operating procedures. If you take the time to memorize the steps for dealing with even an unexpected situation ahead of time, you will feel more prepared to handle that situation should it arise while you are on the job.

3. Learn to recognize the physical signs of stress. These can include:

Tense muscles

Clenched teeth

Making fists or clenching objects

Rapid heartbeat

Shaking

Tightness in the stomach or chest

Shallow breathing

Rapid movements

Restlessness, such as drumming fingers, tapping feet, repetitive movements

Tension headache, backache or neck-ache

4. Consciously relax muscles in the face, arms, neck, back and abdomen.

5. Do deep breathing exercises.

6. Close your eyes and count slowly to ten.

7. Remove yourself from the situation for a short time, if possible.

8. Orally express to someone else that you are feeling stressed.

9. Change the physical position of your body. If you have been sitting, stand up and walk around. If you have been standing, sit down and exhale deeply.

10. Stretch and yawn.

11. Tell a joke or envision a humorous scenario, when possible.

12. Carry an object which brings good memories to mind in your pocket, or place it in another location where you will have easy access to it. Tell yourself that seeing that object will automatically decrease the amount of stress that you feel. When possible, take the object out and look at it, or simply place your hand in your pocket and touch the object. Take 20-30 seconds to recall the good memory associated with your object.

Minimize Stress in the Workplace

Reducing the amount of stress you place on yourself and others can help you become more productive and efficient, in your work environment. While many people thrive in high pressure situations, the negative long term impact of working under a great amount of stress has been verified both by medical and mental health experts. Minimizing stress can make you happier, healthier and more confident at work.

Things to Do

1. Create a schedule for your work day.

2. Establish a routine for handling designated tasks.

3. Don't work through breaks or lunch hours.

4. Break large tasks into manageable pieces. (If you have a 50 page report due in ten days, complete 5 pages per day, rather than trying to complete the entire report at one time).

5. Don't procrastinate.

6. Keep lists and make notes to keep from getting mentally bogged down by trying to remember too many details.

7. Stay organized so that you won't need to search for important papers or other items at the last minute.

8. Try to be early for meetings and appointments. Use the extra time to unwind, have a cup of coffee or enjoy a moment of quiet.

9. Establish good working relationships by being open and honest with coworkers. Avoid office gossip and conversations that reflect negative thoughts and attitudes.

10. Don't take on extra work or overextend yourself in other ways.

11. Minimize distractions. If you need to focus on a certain task, close the door, send your phone to voicemail, turn off background noise. Make others aware that you will be occupied for a time, and would prefer not to be disturbed.

12. Create a comfortable work environment.

13. Limit caffeine intake.

14. Celebrate your accomplishments. Even if you have a boss that never

has a kind word to say about your work performance, if you know you have done an excellent job, take the time to congratulate yourself.

Chapter Nine
Techniques for Improving Cognitive Ability

There are a wide range of products; books, video and audio tapes, experimental techniques and educational programs, all of which claim to help increase intelligence and improve cognitive ability. This chapter will present helpful information regarding many of these techniques and methods, including entrainment, brain-training, hypnosis, subliminal messaging, imagery and visualization techniques, even cognitive-enhancing medications. The goal is to provide you with the most accurate and reliable information about the technique, product or program, as well as to encourage further research on the topic.

Brainwave Patterns and Improved Intelligence

Think of the brain as a battery. It uses a variety of chemicals to produce an electrical current. The current is transmitted between neurons in the brain at varying rates, depending on the type of activity we are engaged in. By using electroencephalography, or EEG technology, researchers are able to record and measure the flow of electrical current between neurons in the brain. Early measures of the brain's electrical activity were recorded as rising and falling patterns, similar to those seen in an ocean wave hence the term brainwave.

When measured over a time period (generally twenty to forty minutes) definite patterns of brainwave activity can be identified. These patterns are related directly to the subject's current physical or mental state. Using a Hertz (Hz) measurement scale, researchers have discovered at least five distinct types of brainwave patterns. These wave patterns are identified by recorded Hz levels, or number of "cycles per second".

Brain Wave Frequency Chart

Gamma Waves - The most recently discovered and least commonly occurring brain wave pattern, gamma waves are very high frequency waves, which signify deep thought and high levels of mental activity and awareness. These waves measure 39 Hz to 100 Hz.

Beta waves - Generally dominant in the brain when we are awake, active and alert. Beta waves measure between 13 Hz and 38 Hz.

Alpha waves - Most dominant during times of relaxation and calm. Alpha waves measure between 8 Hz and 13 Hz.

Theta waves - Dominant during times of deep relaxation, visualization, light sleep and pre-sleep. Theta waves measure between 4 Hz and 7 Hz.

Delta waves - Dominant during deep sleep. These waves measure between 2 Hz and 4 Hz.

Brainwave States

Brainwave states are times throughout the day when one brainwave pattern is more active than the others. For example, when we are in deep sleep, we can be said to be in the delta state, or in "delta sleep." On the other hand, when we are calm and relaxed, we may be either in the alpha or theta states, since these brainwave patterns would be most prominent during times of low activity.

Since brainwave patterns are identified as occurring over a range of frequency (rather than a specific number Hz), we can also be said to be in either "high" or "low" forms of that state. Deep meditation, for example, often occurs in low alpha or high theta, which can be measured between 6 and 9 Hz. On the other hand, light sleep and daydreaming will more likely occur in the low theta state which crosses over to the high delta range at 4 Hz. (See brainwave frequency chart).

Multiple Waves

All of these brainwave patterns are continuously demonstrated in the human brain. Dominant wave patterns emerge however, and change in correlation to, changes in levels of physical and mental activity.

For example, when we are in deep sleep, delta waves may be dominant. On the other hand, we also have varying levels of beta, alpha and theta waves, all of which can become more dominant than delta waves, even though we are asleep.

Using Knowledge of Brainwave Patterns to Increase Intelligence

Many of the techniques discussed in this chapter of the book help to produce desired brain wave patterns, to increase intelligence, improve cognitive ability, increase focus and memory and allow for improvement in other areas of thinking. Most of these techniques take advantage of the alpha and theta states, which some claim are the doorway between the conscious and subconscious minds.

Meditation and Intelligence

Possibly the most effective and inexpensive means of improving intelligence, daily meditation has been shown by researchers at Wake Forest University to improve cognitive abilities and increase academic test scores. Other recent studies, conducted at Yale, Harvard, Massachusetts General Hospital, and Massachusetts Tech have also verified physiological changes in the brain, including increased cortical thickness and changes to gray matter in the right hemisphere of the brain, which were directly linked to routine meditation.

Additionally, research from the University of Wisconsin recently showed that monks who have been trained in various methods of meditation produce gamma waves (the brain waves associated with higher levels of thinking and learning) at a rate greater than any which have been previously documented. The production of gamma waves was directly linked to the amount of training the individual had received in meditation, as well as the number of years which the subject had been practicing meditation.

Of particular interest is the fact that those monks who had been using meditation techniques daily for 25 years demonstrated higher levels of gamma wave production than those who had been practicing for 15 years. This study suggests that there is an unlimited potential for growth in the area of intelligence. The implication may be that the brain can continue to improve cognitive abilities and increase higher thought processes, with continued meditative practice. If the same monks were tested again in 5 years, even those with the most experience would be likely to show further increases in brain activity, after the additional amount of time spent in daily meditation.

A variety of further research suggests that many of the benefits from daily meditation are immediate. It has long been understood that meditation can have a calming effect on both body and mind, improving focus and concentration, while reducing stress and minimizing the effects of fatigue. In 2009, researchers at George Mason University also demonstrated immediate improvement in visuospatial tasks. The prevailing research suggests that significant cognitive improvement can be seen after only a few days of meditation, which lasts for at least 20 minutes. Physiological changes to the brain may take longer to manifest, and may require up to 40 minutes of daily meditation.

Meditation Techniques

While research has not currently explored a wide variety of meditative techniques, both the mindfulness and insight meditation techniques have been used in the above research, with positive results.

Mindfulness is a simple meditative technique which involves focusing on the breathe, while repeating a simple phrase or saying, or calling a specific image to mind. In mindfulness meditation, simply allow the thoughts to flow freely, and do not attempt to push them away. Practicing this simple meditative technique for at least 20 minutes a day has been documented to have a positive effect on both mind and body.

Insight meditation, otherwise referred to as Vipassana, involves directing the focus of the mind onto the body. This type of meditation involves sitting in a comfortable, upright position, and allowing your thoughts to rest on various areas of your body, usually beginning at the top of the head and moving downward slowly. Tensed muscles should be relaxed, and you should take note of any physical sensations you experience, heat, cold, pain, tingling etc… Rather than attempt to push out intrusive thoughts, simply refocus the attention on the body.

A Note about Transcendental Meditation

While transcendental meditation is one of the most well-known forms of meditation, it should be noted that this type of meditation has not been shown to have any greater effect on mental or physical processes, than other forms of meditation. This is especially important since, to become a "true practitioner" of transcendental meditation, a person is required to spend a great deal of money to receive their "personal mantra" and guided instructions.

Entrainment Techniques

Entrainment uses sound, or magnetic resonance to produce frequencies which alter brain waves. The theory behind entrainment is that the brain often tends to "lock-on" to certain frequencies when they are heard or otherwise experienced. When frequencies of a certain Hz are introduced, the brain attempts to follow those frequencies, thereby producing brainwaves which match the designated Hz level. In this way entrainment can cause the brain to create desired wave patterns, whether beta, alpha, theta or delta.

Using sound or magnetic frequencies, a person participating in an entrainment experience can direct the creation of desired brainwave activity. Entrainment can be used for improving concentration and focus, as well as increasing cognitive abilities. It is also commonly used to help achieve the alpha and theta states, to improve relaxation, aid in meditation and visualization techniques, or merely to help induce sleep.

Sine brainwave entrainment serves to help balance the right and left hemispheres of the brain, directing them to produce similar wave patterns. This type of entrainment often provides the participant with a sense of well being and a greater sense of clarity and focus. To achieve this balance, headphones are used, and a slightly different frequency is played into each ear. Little research has been done in clinical settings, regarding the effectiveness of Sine type entrainment techniques.

On the other hand, a great deal of research has been done on single frequency entrainment, as well as magnetic frequency entrainment. Ongoing research is also exploring the effects of various frequency levels, with new trials focusing on high frequency transmissions, over 39 Hz.

It is interesting to note that while participating in experiments conducted at the Monroe Institute, Ken Eagle Feather claims to have discovered many new levels of reality, through experimentation with brainwave altering frequencies. Whether these realities are truly "realities" or simply hallucinations created by the altered brainwave states, is purely speculative. The Monroe Institute itself is a for profit organization, which does not adhere entirely to accepted scientific practices in research and documentation.

Another interesting note on brainwave frequency altering devices, New York Times reporter Lawrence Osborne participated in a single experiment at the University of Sydney. The experiment showed that transcranial magnetic simulators may have the potential to radically alter intelligence levels. In his published account of the experiment, "Savant for a Day", Osborne describes his experience with pencil drawing. He relates that over the course of about ten minutes, while being exposed to the "Medtronic Mag Pro Transcranial Magnetic Simulator", his artistic skills increased exponentially. He links this transformation to an increased ability to visualize details, which he had been previously unable to recall. The effects were not permanent; however at this time it has not been determined if repeated exposure to magnetic entrainment can assist in "training" the brain to operate at this higher level of awareness, continually.

There are many free online single frequency entrainment videos and audios. Brainwaveentrainment.co provides links to free videos, and includes resources for videos which transmit frequencies that may be helpful in improving concentration, as well as those which assist the listener in entering deeper relaxation states and those which can aid in inducing deep sleep.

Image-Streaming

Image streaming is a mental technique which involves visualizing images in your mind, and describing them in vivid detail. The process of image-streaming helps to increase visuospatial skills, and can also enhance other cognitive abilities, when practiced over time. One of the most notable studies to be done on this technique was conducted by Dr. Charles P. Reinert, at Southwest State University. SSU offered a 4 credit hour course on image-streaming to University students. Students enrolled in the course were tested before and after learning and practicing the image-streaming technique. Results showed high levels of improvement in cognitive abilities, with the greatest differences correlating directly to the number of hours the student spent practicing the image-streaming technique.

To practice this technique, sit in a quiet place. Close your eyes and allow your thoughts to flow freely. When an image comes into your mind, immediately begin to describe it. This is best done out loud, whether you choose to share the image with another person, record it for your own personal reference or simply speak your description out loud, for no-one else's benefit.

Continue to focus on the image, and strive to visualize it in as much detail as possible. Notice textures, colors, size, shape and any other features of the image. Rotate the image, or view it from another perspective, for example turn it upside down, sideways or view it at an angle. An image streaming session should last no less than 10 minutes, and may continue up to thirty minutes.

Evaluate and reflect on the image. What is its significance in your life? Is there metaphorical or symbolic meaning to the image? Often the image you receive during an image-streaming session will have an important connection to something else in your life. Many believe that image-streaming allows the conscious and subconscious minds to communicate visually. For more information on understanding your images read "*A Method for Personal Growth and Development*" by Win Wenger or "*The Einstein Factor*" by Wenger and Poe.

Lucid Dreaming

Another technique for improving intelligence, which also focuses on linking the conscious and subconscious minds, and takes advantage of a low frequency brainwave state, lucid dreaming involves controlling dreams with the conscious mind. While many are skeptical of the concept, lucid dreaming has been documented by researchers, and can be identified in a scientific setting. In 1975 the first lucid dream was documented in such a setting. Researchers Keith Hearne and Alan Wosley predetermined a set of eye movements, prior to Wosley entering the dream state. Once in the dream state, Wosley was able to demonstrate the pattern of eye movements, as had been arranged before sleep. This experiment was the first to demonstrate the possibility of remaining consciously aware, while at the same time being completely asleep. More recently, experiments conducted by the Neurological Laboratory in Frankfurt, Germany, have shown that a lucid dream is characterized by a high number of gamma waves, or brainwaves which measure above 38 Hz.

Many people have never experienced a lucid dream. Yet Steven Leberge of Stanford University, an expert in the field of lucid dreams, suggests that it is possible for everyone to dream in this fashion. Leberge states that there are several techniques to help induce lucid dreaming, many of which require little effort or expense.

1. In order to know when you are dreaming, first make a point to realize when you are awake. Leberge suggests a simple test, such as touching the fingers of one hand to the palm of the other. While performing this test ask "Am I awake?" The principle behind this concept is to train the mind to ask whether it is awake or dreaming. By repeating this process a dozen or more times daily, you will be likely to replay the scenario in your dreams, at which time you will realize that you are not awake.

2. Leberge suggests a simple meditative technique which should be done before falling asleep. The technique involves relaxing the physical body, and counting backwards from 100. As you count down, repeat the phrase "I am dreaming" after each decreasing number.

3. Another technique for inducing lucid dreaming is to set your alarm clock to wake you up after you have had four to five hours of normal sleep. Since most people experience lucid dreams after they have had several hours of uninterrupted, normal sleep, waking yourself up and then attempting to direct your continued dreaming, can also help you enter the lucid dream state.

4. Following a period of deep relaxation, try setting the scene for a lucid dream. Create a vivid, detail oriented backdrop of the scene. You may also want to try imagining sounds, rather than pictures. As you immerse yourself in the dream scene, you will begin to lose touch with your physical body. Explore the scene, and feel yourself enter it.

Once you have entered a lucid dream, you are able to control what happens. Many people use lucid dreaming as a way to communicate with the subconscious mind. In his book "Lucid Dreaming; Gateway to the Inner Self" Robert Waggoner suggests simply shouting out a question to your subconscious mind. The answer can appear in many forms, written, spoken, or presented in images. Waggoner also advises directing the dream orally, by shouting out instructions to the subconscious. You may say "Show me something amazing" or "Show me something that is important for me to know." You can find a list of ten subconscious directives for lucid dreaming at theworldofluciddreaming.com

Subliminal and Subconscious Messaging Myths

Did you know that the presence of the smell of cleaning solution may cause you to be neater? Or that the presence of a briefcase in a room can cause you to become more competitive and business minded? How about the fact that your impressions of a random stranger may be totally different, depending on whether she asks you to hold a hot or a cold drink? According to an article in the New York Times, "Who's Minding the Mind"? (Carey, 2007) the subconscious really does a play a huge role in our everyday decisions and observations.

Does this mean that if we spray cleaning solution in our homes in the morning we will be more likely to feel motivated to clean the house for the rest of the day? Not really. Once the conscious mind becomes aware of what is happening, it no longer works to guide your decisions in the same way.

Maybe you are familiar with the story about Coke's subliminal message experiment, which took place in a movie theater in 1957. Some versions of that story have consumers flocking to the concession stands in record numbers, compelled to buy a Coke. In truth, however, the experiment and its remarkable results were later determined to be entirely fraudulent. Yet, there is still a wide range of products on the market today, including video and audio programs that promise miraculous results using subliminal or subconscious messaging.

Are subliminal messages, words, images or sounds which appear below our level of conscious processing, really a good way to program the subconscious mind? Most recent studies say no. The whole point of a "subliminal" message is that it is does not register in the conscious mind. Once the conscious mind takes control of the "programming" however, it tends not to work. Before investing in a series of subliminal audio or video programs, then, it may be to your benefit to investigate other options for working with your subconscious mind, to either improve intelligence, or make other lasting mental or behavioral changes.

NLP: The basics of Neuro-Linguistic Programming

Neuro-Linguistic Programming can be seen as a combination of many different beliefs, techniques and approaches to self-improvement. NLP seeks to identify patterns in thought, speech and behavior, which can be altered for increased communication, awareness and understanding. It is often used conjointly with other techniques, such as hypnosis, entrainment and accelerated learning methods.

According to the book _NLP, the New Technology of Achievement_ (Andreas, Faulkner et al, 1996) the term Neuro-linguistic programming is defined by the idea that the human brain operates like a computer, and will run whatever program it is conditioned by experience and perception to run. The programs that the brain "turns on" at any given time can be identified by patterns in thought, behavior and speech. NLP is based on the idea that the mind's current programs can be changed only by reprogramming the brain itself. As Albert Einstein once said "Insanity is doing the same thing over and over, and attempting to get a different result." NLP assumes that people will run the same program repeatedly, unless they are somehow introduced to a new programming model.

New "programs" are introduced in a variety of ways. One of the most notable uses of NLP is that it enables people to be introduced to new behavior and language models. Using well-known role models, experts in a particular field, NLP incorporates speech and thinking patterns from these individuals into its "reprogramming" materials.

NLP is closely related to quantum psychology, in that it promotes the idea that "you are what you think you are." If you study and learn the thinking patterns of a successful individual, you are able to become that individual; to not only learn to walk and talk as they do, but to think and behave in the same manner as well.

NLP is often used in conjunction with hypnosis, to help participants assimilate new language and behavior patterns quickly. It is also often associated with photo-reading and accelerated learning techniques, sometimes called "super-learning."

Paraliminal messaging, in the form of audio CD's, is also used in conjunction with NLP. A combination of entrainment and positive affirmations, paraliminal messaging uses voice, words and language patterns, as well as entrainment music, to help reprogram the brain.

There has been very little research on the effectiveness of NLP alone. This is because NLP utilizes many previously documented ideas and theories, as part of its own programs. It is also because techniques employed by NLP, such as hypnosis and quantum psychology, are often studied apart from NLP's particular application of the technique.

Brain-Training Websites, Downloads and Game Consoles

Throughout this book the idea of exercise for the mind has been a prominent idea. Since the brain is like a muscle, routine exercise is a necessary part of keeping it healthy and functioning properly.

Modern technology has brought with it the concept of "brain-exercise" programs, many of which claim to increase intelligence and improve cognitive ability, when used routinely. Websites that require a monthly subscription or a one time only fee, to access "brain games" are becoming relatively common. There is little evidence to support the benefits of subscribing to this type of website, however. While some studies suggest that computer simulated games with a real world application can increase speed of processing and visuospatial skills, especially in the elderly population, there is little evidence that repeated exposure to an online "brain exercise" will have any real world application for increased intelligence.

When thinking about "brain training exercises" keep in mind that most researchers agree what matters most is that you keep the brain active and engaged. Rather than repeatedly replaying the same types of scenarios on a computer screen or game console, experts suggest that you continue to explore new concepts, ideas and try new activities.

The important word is new. Once you become familiar with a task and have mastered the basic elements of that task, the continuing benefits are most likely limited. While there is still much research to be done in this area, and there may be benefits from routine and repeated exposure to these types of activities which are as yet undocumented, you may reap more benefits by engaging in a wide range of traditional activities. Playing checkers, chess and some forms of solitaire may have as much benefit as subscribing to a website which offers "brain training".

On the other side of that argument, however, exposure to new ideas and activities through these types of sites can have a positive effect, if you make it a point to expose yourself to a wide range of activities. Rather than trying to improve thinking in one specific area, with "memory training" or "analytical thinking" games for example, approach such activities as new and interesting experiences. Seek to understand the underlying concept of the game, but don't get stuck in a routine of replaying a certain one trying to get better at it.

Try to incorporate a real world application to the brain training experience. In order for tacit knowledge to be converted to practical intelligence, we need to experiment with using any new skills or abilities in everyday life. After engaging in a "brain training" activity consider how that activity can help you in life. Make an effort to relate the experience to work or everyday events. This will help you retain any knowledge you gained while engaging in the activity.

Cognitive Enhancing Medications

Many professionals are turning to cognitive enhancing medications, otherwise known as <u>nootropics</u>, to increase concentration and heighten mental abilities. These drugs can have a positive impact on mental performance, enabling you to think more clearly and maintain focus for longer periods of time. Some types of cognitive enhancing drugs have also been shown to increase memory and recall ability, making them popular "study-aids." Unlike many other types of drugs, <u>nootropics</u> may also help improve judgment, and enhance decision making abilities, as well.

Adderall, Ritalin and Modafinil (Provigil or Alertec) are the most commonly used "smart drugs." All require a prescription and most are difficult to obtain without a verified medical condition. Yet, a great number of scientists, executives and other professionals are taking these types of medications to enhance their work performance, and meet the demands of an increasingly competitive work environment.

On the downside, these drugs can have serious side effects on both physical and mental health. Some of the more commonly used cognitive enhancing drugs have been associated with psychotic behavior and can cause insomnia, paranoia and a realm of other mental health problems. The drugs have been shown to increase blood pressure as well, which can lead to more health complications, such as heart attack and stroke.

When taken under the close supervision of a doctor, however, nootropics may have fewer complications and less side effects than many other commonly prescribed medications. Some medical professionals condone the use of cognitive enhancing drugs, especially for middle aged people, who work in some type of high pressure industry. If you plan to use these drugs to enhance cognitive abilities, be honest with your doctor, and discuss the possible benefits as well as the potential risks, before using any of these medications.

Chapter Ten
Diet, Nutrition and Intelligence

The human brain is a highly complex organ. As such, the brain requires a complex combination of substances, vitamins, minerals, acids and other naturally occurring substances, to keep it functioning at peak efficiency. The lack of any one essential substance can cause a range of cognitive problems, from difficulty concentrating to memory loss or memory impairment.

According to the American Academy of Neurology, a diet which includes fresh fruits and vegetables, fish and shellfish, nuts, seeds and omega 3 fatty acids can help to improve brain health, as well as cognitive ability. It may also lessen the risk of Alzheimers and help to prevent brain shrinkage. Additionally, eating foods high in omega 3 fatty acids, along with foods that are rich in vitamins B, C, E and D can help prevent a decline in mental performance, which is often associated with aging.

Fatty Acids and Brain Function

You may not realize that two-thirds of the human brain is composed of fatty acids. Docosahexaenoic acid, or DHA, an omega 3 fatty acid, is the most commonly occurring acid within the brain, and is a primary component of the plasma membrane that surrounds the neuron. This acid plays a vital role in neurotransmission and synaptic function. A deficiency in DHA has been linked to ADHD, Alzheimers and a general cognitive decline.

The best source of this omega 3 fatty acid is the consumption of cold-water fish and shellfish. Salmon, herring, tuna and mackerel are all considered good sources of this omega 3 fatty acid. Fish oil caplets and other DHA supplements are also an acceptable way to add more of this fatty acid to the diet. When taking nutritional supplements, however, it is advised that you look for those which contain higher amounts of DHA, as opposed to EPA, a fatty acid that does not occur naturally in the brain. Since many supplements contain a combination of the two fatty acids, be sure to read the label carefully, before making a selection.

Other important fatty acids that may also help to improve cognitive function, include linoleic acid (LA) and alpha-linolenic acid (ALA). Increasing intake of these fatty acids may help to improve memory and concentration, and improve over all brain function. The best sources include seeds, nuts, fish and shellfish, as well as non-hydrogenated oils such as flax seed oil, safflower oil, and soybean oil.

Since saturated and trans-fatty acids interfere with the function of polyunsaturated fatty acids in the omega 3, 6 and 9 groups, it is important that trans and saturated fats be consumed in small amounts. Trans fatty acids are found in red meat, eggs, dairy products, margarine, hydrogenated oils and products made with these ingredients.

ORAC and Brain Health

According to the USDA a number of laboratory studies, conducted by Joseph A. Jones of the Human Nutrition Research Center, at Tufts University, have recently demonstrated important links between antioxidant compounds, in the form of plant extracts, and brain health. These studies have shown that when fed to laboratory rats, blueberry, strawberry and spinach extracts reversed age related cognitive impairments, increased learning and memory ability in rats who already had signs of plaque within the brain, and also increased signs of neuro-genesis, or neuron regeneration.

According to the report, the oxygen radical absorbance capacity (ORAC) of a plant food has a direct bearing on its ability to impact brain health. The ORAC score is a measure of a plants antioxidant effect.

The best sources for antioxidant rich nutrition include fruits, vegetables, whole grains, nuts and seeds. Since plant foods are rich in a wide range of vitamins and minerals, and researchers do not have a clear understanding of how various nutrients work together within the body and brain, it is important that plant foods be consumed in their natural form, to obtain the greatest nutritional benefits.

Vitamins C, E, D and B

While the presence of vitamins C, E, D as well as several B vitamins, are essential to brain health and peak cognitive performance, deficiencies can result in cognitive impairment, and even long term brain damage. In the previously mentioned experiments, vitamin E, a powerful antioxidant, is thought to play a large role in observed nuerogenesis and improved cognitive abilities.

Vitamin C, also known as ascorbic acid, is another powerful antioxidant. It is essential to brain health and is known to help protect healthy cells from damage by free radicals. Adults need between 75 mg and 90 mg of vitamin C daily, for optimal physical and mental health. Smokers should include an additional 35 mg of vitamin C in the daily diet, to compensate for a greater number of free radicals in the body.

Vitamin D is used by the nerves, and is required to maintain healthy communication between the body and brain. To process vitamin D efficiently, daily exposure to sunlight is also necessary. Most adults require 600 iu of vitamin D, to maintain healthy levels in the body. Vitamin D deficiency is one of the most common vitamin deficiencies in the U.S.

Contrary to popular belief, all dairy products are not good sources of this essential vitamin. While most milk is fortified with D vitamins, cheese, ice cream and other dairy products are generally not. The best sources of Vitamin D include fatty fish, such as tuna, sardines and salmon, fortified cereal, fortified orange juice and milk, and yogurt.

For brain health, also consider increasing your intake of vitamin B12, B6 and B3, otherwise known as niacin. B12 helps to maintain healthy nerves and blood cells, while B6 is essential to healthy brain development and enzyme reactions. Vitamin B3 or B6 deficiencies can cause concentration difficulties, confusion, poor memory, anxiety, loss of interest and irritability.

Vitamin B9, or Folic acid, is essential to the production of DNA and RNA, as well as for healthy cell division. A deficiency in folate can cause forgetfulness, confusion and behavioral disorders. The recommended daily allowance of this B vitamin is 400 micrograms for most adults. Folic acid is best obtained through natural food sources such as avocado, lentils, spinach, beans and seeds. Before adding a supplement of folic acid to your diet, consult a physician. Excess folic acid can mask other vitamin deficiencies, causing difficulty in their treatment and diagnosis.

Other Essential Nutrients

Iodine deficiency can result in lower than average IQ scores. The lack of this nutrient can also decrease an adult's ability to work and think clearly. The recommended daily allowance for iodine is 150 mg. Iodine deficiency in the U.S. was addressed when manufacturers of salt first started producing "Iodized" salt. For those who are cutting down on salt intake, however, iodine deficiency may be more of concern. If your current consumption of iodized salt is not sufficient to meet the daily requirements, boost consumption of fish, shellfish, grains and breads. Discuss your concerns with a doctor or other medical professional, before taking an iodine supplement, however, as too much iodine can be toxic.

Iron deficiency is considered to be the leading nutritional disorder, both in the United States and around the world. An estimated eighty percent of people worldwide are iron deficient. The lack of this nutrient can result in fatigue and poor work performance. It is necessary for the transportation of oxygen throughout the body, for healthy cell growth and for many essential biochemical reactions. Iron can be found in found in two distinct forms, heme iron, which is found in meats and non-heme iron, which is derived from plant life. Heme iron is more readily absorbed by the body, and can be found in chicken liver, oysters and beef liver. Non heme iron is found in fortified cereals and oatmeal, a variety of beans, tofu and spinach.

General Health and Nutrition, and Intelligence

Eating regular, healthy meals is important to cognitive ability. Three studies by David Benton and Pearl Y. Parker, published in the American Journal of Clinical Nutrition, demonstrate a drop in cognitive performance and recall abilities in school children who missed breakfast. The same response can be found in adults who skip meals, later experiencing a decline in blood glucose levels. Missing meals can make it difficult to concentrate, and you may also have more trouble recalling key concepts.

Eat foods that contain enough carbohydrates to fuel the body and brain. According to the USDA low carbohydrate diets can have a detrimental impact on cognitive function, especially in areas related to memory and recall ability. Dieters were asked to participate in a special study before beginning and again three weeks after beginning low carb-dieting. Memory test scores decreased significantly, following limited carbohydrate intake. Scores improved again, once dieters were reintroduced to a normal carbohydrate intake.

Add soy to your diet. According to the article "Soy Appears to Benefit Cognitive Function", written by Sandra E. File, Ph.D, director of the Psychopharmacology Research Unit, Centre for Neuroscience, King's College London, a diet rich in soy and soy based products can have a positive impact on cognitive ability. A compilation of three recent studies on the benefits of soy shows that this health food can have a positive impact on immediate and short term memory and recall abilities, as well as on frontal lobe function. Eating more tofu, soybeans, soy milk and soy nuts, or adding soy protein supplements to your diet may be a good way to increase cognitive ability.

Eating foods that are high in sugar may also have a detrimental impact on cognitive performance. A sugary snack may be able to give you a quick pick up, but once the sugar burns off you will most likely have an even more difficult time with focus and concentration. Instead of a refined sugar snack, try fruit and natural fruit juices, which can give you the same feeling of a quick pick up, without the adverse affects later.

Consider adding a multivitamin to your diet. Since the body and brain require a wide range of nutrients to function normally, even those who strive to eat a diet consisting of natural, healthy foods may be able to benefit from the supplemental nutrition provided by a multivitamin. Depending on your gender, age, dietary needs and overall health, your doctor can help you determine which multivitamin can provide the most nutritional benefits.

Other Things to Do

1. Avoid refined and processed foods.

2. Opt for natural, fresh foods as often as possible.

3. Eat a variety of raw fruits, vegetables, nuts and seeds.

4. Select whole grain cereals and breads. Look for whole grain varieties of rice, pasta and noodles.

5. Eat fresh foods as soon after buying them as possible. This helps ensure optimal nutritional value.

6. Avoid canned, boxed and other types of prepackaged meals.

7. Stay away from preservatives, artificial colors and artificial sweeteners.

8. Eat several times throughout the day to help maintain proper levels of glucose and restore depleted carbohydrate levels.

9. Drink a cup of brewed herbal tea daily.

10. Drink alcohol in moderation.

11. Eat dark chocolate in moderation. It can increase dopamine and serotonin levels, giving you a needed boost.

12. Consult your doctor or other medical professional before making changes to your diet and nutritional program. They are best placed to assess your current health, make recommendations and track your progress.

Closing Thoughts

This book was written to provide you with useable information, with no fluff or filler, and its clearly a no nonsense guide to improving intelligence. When you look back over this book you`ll see we have covered a tremendous number of practical recommendations you can act on. You also have links to relevant resources and a reference section at the back of the book. So, what is the best course of action at this point?

Go back to page 1 and take a chapter at a time. Reread each section, takes notes and put the training to good use at work. Bear in mind, you are learning new ways of thinking and behaving so some conditioning is necessary. Changes won`t happen immediately simply because you understand the concepts. You MUST apply the training to see noticeable changes in how you think. Practice these new skills and you will become smarter, faster and more creative at work!